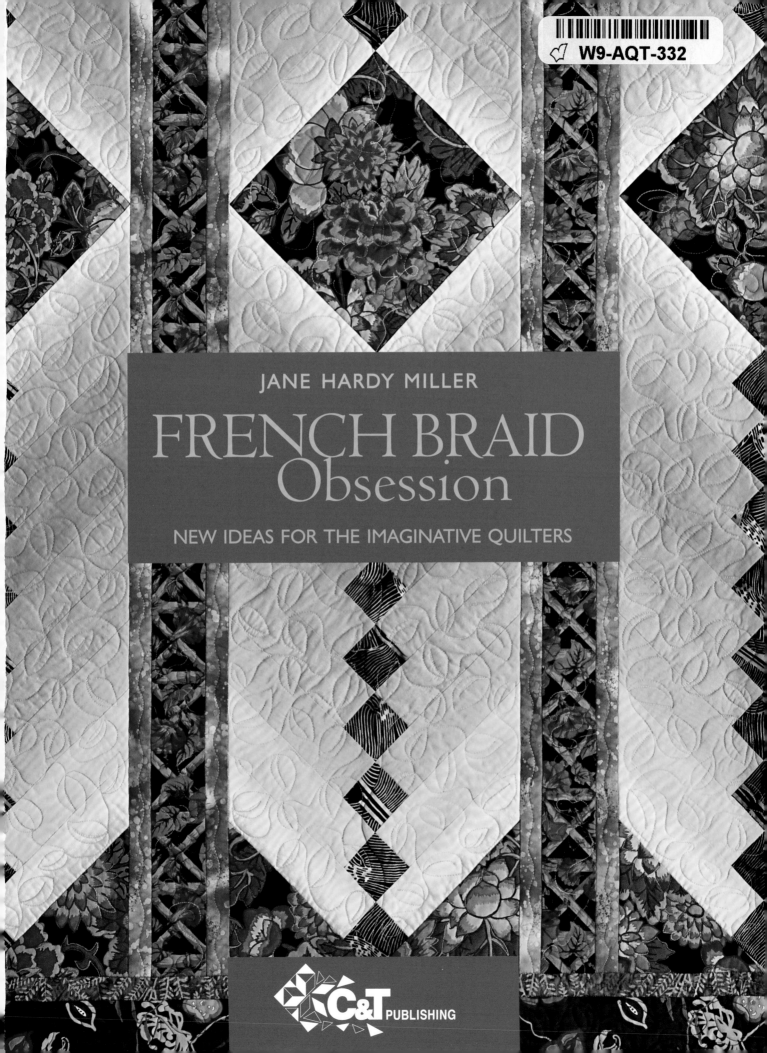

JANE HARDY MILLER

FRENCH BRAID
Obsession

NEW IDEAS FOR THE IMAGINATIVE QUILTERS

C&T PUBLISHING

Text copyright © 2009 by Jane Hardy Miller

Artwork copyright © 2009 by C&T Publishing, Inc.

Publisher: *Amy Marson*

Creative Director: *Gailen Runge*

Editor: *Liz Aneloski*

Technical Editors: *Carolyn Aune and Rebekah Genz*

Copyeditor/Proofreader: *Wordfirm Inc.*

Cover Designer: *Kristen Yenche*

Book Designer: *Rose Sheifer-Wright*

Production Coordinator: *Tim Manibusan*

Illustrator: *Tim Manibusan*

Photography by *Christina Carty-Francis and Diane Pedersen* of C&T Publishing, Inc., unless otherwise noted

Published by C&T Publishing, Inc., P.O. Box 1456, Lafayette, CA 94549

Library of Congress Cataloging-in-Publication Data
Miller, Jane Hardy
French braid obsession : new ideas for the imaginative quilter / Jane Hardy Miller.
    p. cm.
Summary: "Eight quilt projects using the step-by-step instructions given for making French braid quilts. Basic quilting instructions also included"--Provided by publisher.
ISBN 978-1-57120-526-1 (paper trade : alk. paper)
1. Quilting--Patterns. I. Title.
TT835.M5134 2009
746.46'041--dc22
                                        2008036073
Printed in China
10 9 8 7 6 5

CONTENTS

Dedication

This book is dedicated to Farren Briana Miller and Travis Valerian Miller. No mother could be luckier—or more grateful—than I to have such wonderful children with such good hearts.

Acknowledgments

It is a paradox of writing that although a writer writes alone, no book is written by only one person. I am fortunate to have had a great deal of support during the creation of this book. Denise Scalon was kind enough to sew experimental braids for me, and she and Amy Cohn both graciously made quilt labels on demand. My bosses, Lucy and Eddie Mansfield, were unflagging in their encouragement and tech support, both mental and mechanical, and Joan Bailey McMath was again my first and best proofreader.

Patricia Ritter and Robin Fouquette improved the book (by allowing me to use their quilts) as did my editors, Liz Aneloski and Carolyn Aune, who provided constant encouragement and instantaneous responses to my questions. Last but by no means least, I am grateful to Arlene Netten, whose pattern Fabulous Florals was the starting point for every braid that followed.

Introduction

Quilters who have made log cabin quilts know how quickly they can be put together, and French braid quilts are nothing more than two-sided log cabins. There's quite a bit of design flexibility with the braids and their various permutations, and the construction is deceptively simple. The only challenging part of the process is fabric selection. If you're insecure about that, there are always friends and quilt shop employees to assist you. In fact, total strangers are frequently eager to offer opinions.

The quilts in this book are a bit different from those in its predecessor, *French Braid Quilts*. That book focused on basic braids, their separators, and the art of combining the two components. Although all the projects in this book are grounded in basic French braids, they tend to fall into one of two categories. There are quilts that use the fabric or the braids in a nontraditional way or that alter the braids in some way, and there are the border quilts.

I had been making French braid quilts for several years and had begun to fear that I'd exhausted the possibilities. Then it occurred to me that the braids could be used as borders, and new and exciting possibilities came to mind. The recent, coincidental trend in the manufacturing sector toward large prints—some so large that they're difficult to use other than as backs or borders—added inspiration. One solution was to use the big print—fabric that you really don't want to cut into anyway—by framing it with French braid borders. The borders are French braids and the center is one piece of fabric. What could be easier?

I'm excited to still be having fun with French braids. I hope you'll feel the same.

French braid quilts are nothing more than two-sided log cabins.

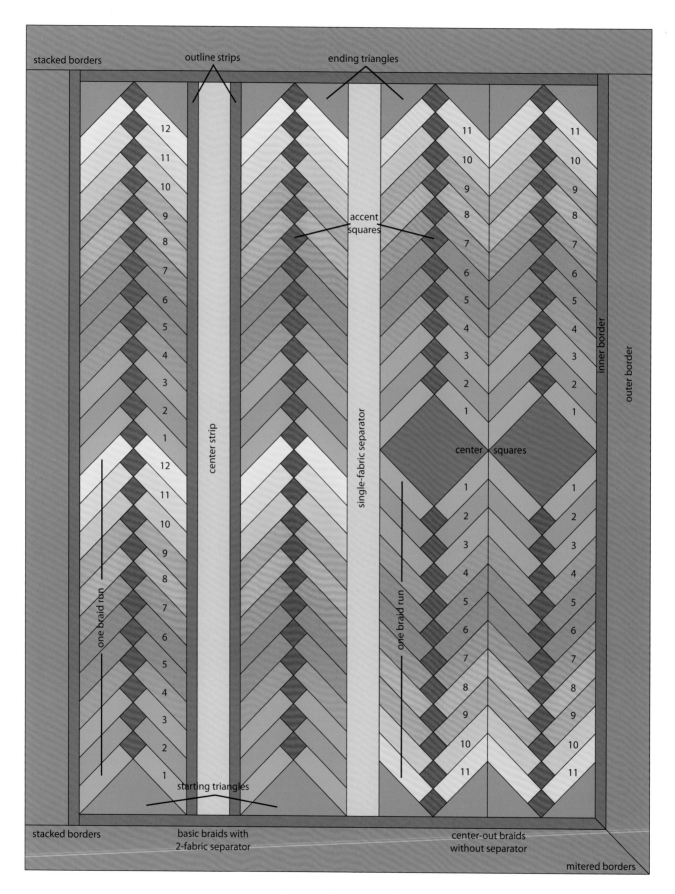

Anatomy of a French Braid

Basics

Equipment

To make any of the quilts in this book, you will need a sewing machine in good working condition and basic sewing equipment: scissors, seam ripper, ironing board, and iron. Good-quality, 50-weight cotton thread and a new sewing machine needle—I use Schmetz Microtex, size 70/10—will also make a difference in your finished product. Thin, sharp pins are also essential; I prefer silk pins, as the tiny heads make it possible to place a rotary ruler on top of them without rocking the ruler while cutting. (Note: In photos throughout this book, larger pins have been used only for visibility.)

A 45mm or 60mm rotary cutter, a self-healing mat, and a 24″ × 6″ (or 6½″) ruler are required for most projects. Another ruler 12″ to 14″ long is convenient for cutting smaller segments, and at least one ruler should have a 45°-angle line. An Omnigrid 98L ruler is helpful if you will be fussy cutting starting triangles, but it is not required for most projects. Please remember that rotary cutters can cause serious injuries—*pay attention* while you cut.

For marking on the bias grain of fabric, I prefer mechanical pencils for a uniformly thin line, but be sure to also have on hand your favorite marker for dark fabrics. Don't forget that the outcome of your project requires accurate measuring and cutting, as well as straight seams with consistent ¼″ seam allowances.

Appliqué

If you have a favorite among the many techniques for hand or machine appliqué, by all means use it. If you intend to blindstitch appliqué by machine, try the following method, which works well on medium to large pieces and for less extreme shapes.

1. Draw the reverse of your finished shape onto the paper side of fusible web and cut on the line.

2. Following the manufacturer's instructions, press this shape onto the back of the fabric to be appliquéd.

3. Cut out the fabric around the pressed shape, leaving a seam allowance. The size of the seam allowance depends on the fabric. I prefer to leave about ³⁄₁₆″ (halfway between ⅛″ and ¼″), but fabrics with a looser weave may require slightly larger seam allowances. Use slightly smaller seam allowances on convex curves for ease of turning.

4. To reduce bulk, clip the concave inner curves and inner points of the seam allowances and notch the convex outer curves almost to the stitching line. Trim diagonally across any outside corners, leaving about ⅛″ beyond the stitching line.

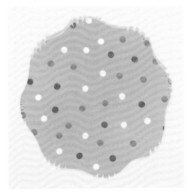

Clip and notch appliqué pieces.

5. Use the paper edge of the fusible web as a rigid edge to press the seam allowance to the back of the appliqué. Fold over the fabric with your fingers just ahead of the tip of the iron.

Use iron tip to press seam allowance over paper's edge.

6. Carefully remove the paper from the back of the appliqué.

7. Use the tip of your iron to fuse **only the seam allowance** to the back of the appliqué, this time adhering it to the fusible web. Refold the seam allowance with your fingertips just ahead of the iron if necessary. Do not press past the seam allowance or you will fuse the piece to your iron. (If this happens, clean the soleplate with hot-iron cleaner before continuing.)

Remove paper and fuse seam allowance.

8. Press the shape in place onto your background and blind-stitch around the edge, pinning the very edge if necessary.

Note

If you decide to stack appliqué shapes, as in the flowers in *Braid in Bloom* (page 30), start with the top shape, often a flower center. Appliqué it to an oversized piece of the fabric that will appear beneath it, then decide on the exact placement of the second shape on the under fabric. Again draw the reverse shape onto the fusible web, apply the fusible web to the second piece, and cut the next shape, leaving a seam allowance for turning.

Follow Steps 5–8 to complete that shape and continue for each subsequent layer.

Borders

Most quilters use butted (lapped) borders because of ease of construction. The main drawback of these borders is that the quilt must be remeasured after each pair of border pieces is added. The following method has worked well for me when applying multiple butted borders. These directions assume that you are adding 1″ inner and 4″ outer borders; adjust the instructions for other sizes.

Multiple Stacked Borders

1. Measure the width (the shorter dimension) across the center of the quilt top. Cut 2 pieces of inner border fabric to that measurement by 1½″ wide. Piece strips end to end if necessary to obtain the required length.

2. Mark the centers of the inner borders and top edges. Match the ends and centers of the borders to the ends and centers of the top; sew. Press the seams toward the borders.

3. Measure the resulting length (the longer dimension) down the center of the quilt top and multiply by 2. Add 2″ to 3″ for insurance. Cut a piece of inner border fabric the resulting measurement by 1½″ wide; cut a piece of outer border fabric the resulting measurement by 4½″ wide. Piece strips end to end if necessary to obtain the required length.

4. Sew together the long sides of the inner and outer border pieces. Press the seams toward the outer border.

5. Cut 2 borders the original length measurement obtained in Step 3 (before you added the extra inches). Sew these borders to the sides of the quilt top, as in Step 2. Press the seams toward the borders.

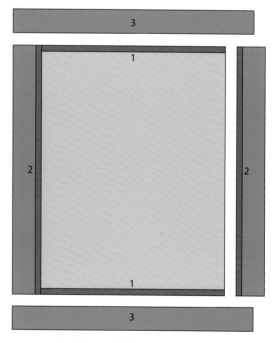

Applying multiple stacked borders

6. Measure the resulting width of the quilt top across the center. Cut 2 pieces of outer border fabric this measurement by 4½″ wide. Piece strips end to end if necessary to obtain the required length. Sew these borders to the top and bottom edges of the quilt top, as in Step 2.

If you are applying more than two borders, continue to add presewn pairs in alternate directions until you finish with the final single pair. Remember that when using this method, the first seam is on the *short sides* of the quilt if you are adding an *even number* of borders (e.g., inner and outer); the first seam is on the *long sides* if you are adding an *odd number* (e.g., inner, middle, outer).

Multiple Stacked Borders with Cornerstones

Occasionally, either as a design element or because of lack of fabric, you may want to add cornerstones to your borders (see, for example, *What Was I Thinking?* page 34). To do so, follow these steps, assuming 1″ inner and 4″ outer finished borders.

1. Follow Steps 1–5 of Multiple Stacked Borders (page 8).

2. Measure across the center of the quilt from the seam that joins the inner and outer borders on one side of the top to the same seam on the other side. Add ½″ to this measurement. Cut your outer crosswise borders the resulting length measurement by 4½″ wide.

3. Cut 4 squares the cut width of the outer border (in this case, 4½″ × 4½″). Sew a square to each end of each crosswise border. Press the seams toward the borders.

4. Sew the crosswise borders to the top and bottom of the quilt, matching corners and ends. Match the cornerstone seams to the seams between the inner and outer borders.

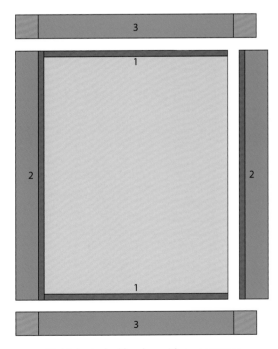

Multiple stacked borders with cornerstones

Mitered Borders

The instructions that follow presuppose a single border. If you are applying multiple borders, they will be progressively longer as you approach the quilt's outer edge (see Step 1 below for determining lengths to cut). Before beginning the mitering process, sew the borders together into a single unit, *matching the centers*. Press the seams in the side border units toward the outer edges and the top and bottom border units toward the inner edges—or vice versa—for later ease in sewing the miter seam. Then complete Steps 2–9 as if your multiple borders were one.

1. Measure the length and width of the center of the quilt top and add 2 times the width of your border, plus an extra 4″, to each measurement. Cut 2 side borders and 2 top and bottom border units to these lengths, piecing strips end to end if necessary to obtain the required length. (If you add other borders, remember to include the width of the previous borders when figuring the subsequent border lengths.)

2. Mark the center points of all 4 borders and all 4 sides of the quilt top in the seam allowances. From the center marks on both side borders, measure out in both directions and mark half of the measured length of the quilt top. From the center marks on the top and bottom borders, measure in both directions and mark half of the measured width of the quilt top.

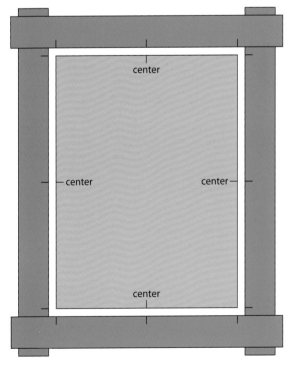

Marking for mitering

3. Pin the marked edges of the side borders to the edges of the quilt top, matching the center marks. Match the outer marks on the border to the edges of the quilt top.

4. Stitch the borders to the sides of the quilt top, starting and stopping at the seam allowance line, ¼" from the edge. Backstitch at both ends. Excess border length will extend beyond each edge. Press the seams toward the borders.

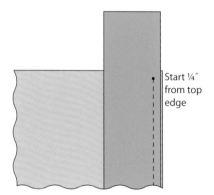

Start ¼" from top edge

Start and stop ¼" from edge of top.

5. Repeat Steps 3 and 4 for the top and bottom borders.

6. To create the miter, lay the quilt top on a table. Fold the quilt, right sides together, through the corner as if making a paper airplane. Pin together the corners and outer edges of the 2 borders. Pin the border seams together, pushing the seam allowances up and out of the way where they meet at the corner.

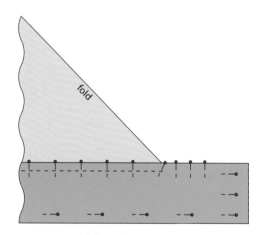

Fold through corner and pin.

7. Position a 45°-45°-90° triangle ruler over the corner, aligning the long side of the ruler with the diagonal fold in the center section of the quilt and the adjacent side of the ruler with the outer edges of the borders. Make sure that the long side of the ruler exactly meets the corner where the seams end. If necessary, adjust the quilt so its edges

are aligned with the triangle ruler. Draw a line for the miter from the end of the border seam to the outer edge of the border.

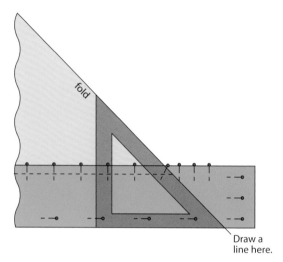

Draw a line here.

Align ruler and mark sewing line.

8. Pin and stitch on the line, backstitching at both ends of the seam. Stitch only up to the border seam, taking care not to stitch the border seam allowances where they have been pinned out of your way. Trim the extra border fabric to ¼".

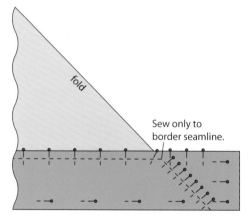

Sew only to border seamline.

Stitch on line.

9. Turn the piece over, spread the miter seam with your fingers, and look at the point where the 3 seams meet. If it is acceptable, press the seam open. If the seams don't appear to meet exactly, try pressing the seam allowances to one side; try doing this in both directions, because one side usually looks better than the other.

Fabric Selection

Fabric selection is the most challenging part of making French braid quilts, and it requires time and patience. Your initial goal is to select fabric for the braid run, the accent squares, and either the starting triangles or the center squares. The braids are a true example of a whole being more than the sum of its parts, so do not attempt to select fabric for the ending triangles, separators, or borders yet—everything will look different after the braids are constructed.

Braid Run

When choosing fabric for the braid run, your goal is for each fabric to blend into the next. Although this sometimes means that two adjacent fabrics are very similar in color or value, the overall look is what matters most, because the viewer's eye usually follows the progression of color rather than seeing each segment individually. Of course, if one particular fabric is much brighter or duller than the others, it will attract the eye, so try to be objective in your choices. Your favorite fabric doesn't have to be included if it serves its purpose as an inspiration for the rest of the braid. Because there will be further fabric selection as you progress, you may be able to use your pet later anyway.

Begin the selection by picking 10 to 12 fabrics for the braid run. It's fine to have a color scheme in mind, as long as you are willing to change that scheme according to fabric availability—this is definitely a go-with-the-flow process. Avoid fabrics that are diagonally patterned in only one direction, because the print will be vertical on one side of the braid and horizontal on the other. Also beware of large, high-contrast prints, which can appear as distracting blotches in the braid segments. Plaids, stripes, and regular designs are fine if you are willing to either cut carefully or ignore the possibility that the design may edge off the sides of the segments. One-way designs can work well if you either take care to ensure that the print faces the same direction on both sides of the braid or ignore the fact that it doesn't. When bolts are stacked, you see the crosswise grain; because the braid segments are cut on the lengthwise grain, however, you should unroll a bit of yardage to make sure that you're seeing what you'll get when you cut.

Lengthwise versus crosswise pattern

Start by selecting 3 or 4 fabrics that work well together. You may eventually reject some or all of these, but it is important to get the run started.

Groups of possible starter fabrics

Walk around the quilt shop—or rifle through your stash—to find others that blend. While continuing the selection process, it will be necessary to eliminate some of the fabrics you have previously picked, because the appearance of the run changes each time you alter the combination. Add, subtract, and rearrange until you are satisfied with the braid run; then stand back about 8 to 10 feet and look again. Make sure that no one fabric attracts your eye immediately and that the colors blend together well.

Braid run selection—start with top fabrics and add fabrics to complete the run.

Accent

When you are satisfied with the braid run, pick an accent color. A smaller, tone-on-tone or geometric print is often best. Remember that the pieces will be placed on the diagonal in the finished quilt. The color is usually one that appears in several of the braid-run fabrics but that also contrasts with most. Don't worry if your accent blends in with a few of your braid fabrics; however, if it blends in with most of them, change it. If you are lucky, you will have several choices; if you are luckier, one will be an obvious winner. If you like more than one possibility, pick one as the front-runner but keep the others available, as you may decide to change the accent once you select your starting triangle fabric.

Starting Triangles or Center Squares

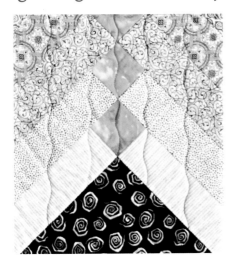

To choose the starting triangle or center square, look for a fabric whose color and print harmonize with most of the braid-run fabrics. The print should be interesting enough to appear as a large-ish piece without overwhelming either the adjacent first fabric in the braid run or the accent square that will adjoin it point to point.

For *starting triangles*, directional prints can work if you are willing to buy extra fabric and to cut carefully (page 17). However, anything that appears in an obvious row, including stripes or plaids, may be askew in the final product. So, yes, buy the fabric with the treetops all pointing one direction, but don't buy the fabric with the trees in perfect orchard configuration.

If you are selecting for a *center square*, you have a bit more latitude. Because you will not be trimming the square later, a geometric could be used with little problem; just remember that whatever you choose will always appear prominently across the middle of the quilt and, if you cut with the grain, it will appear on the diagonal. The piece will lie next to the first fabric in the braid run and will touch the accent squares only at the corner tips. (See page 17 for information on cutting directional fabrics.)

Good choices for starting triangles

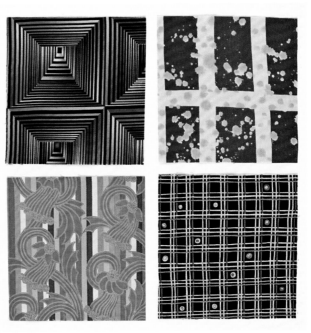

Poor choices for starting triangles

Ending Triangles

After you have sewn your braids, take them back to the quilt shop and select the fabric for the ending triangles. Look for a fabric that contrasts with the last braid-run fabric and the accents but that also complements the other fabrics in the run; include the starting triangle (or center square) fabric in your considerations. Use *only* nondirectional prints for these triangles and remember that they will adjoin the accent fabric. Place any triangle candidate against the end of your braid to make sure that the last braid-run and accent square fabrics are still distinct where the fabrics adjoin.

Separators

It is often possible to pick separators when you choose the ending triangles. These pieces usually consist of outline and center strips, and their effect and selection are similar to those of inner and outer borders on most quilts. Begin by looking for an interesting print or stripe for the center strips, possibly from the same fabric line as one of the braid-run fabrics. If you were forced to discard your favorite fabric from the braid run, now is the time to revisit it.

Outline strips should delineate the braids, so pick a fabric that contrasts with both the braids and the center separators. One of the fabrics that you rejected as an accent can often work well here; sometimes even the accent fabric itself is suitable. Be sure to lay out the braids with your prospective selections to see the effect as a whole.

It is perfectly acceptable to opt for a single-fabric separator, but this selection is often more difficult than choosing a two-fabric version. The most successful single-fabric separators seem to be constructed of fabric that is the same as or very similar to the accent fabric.

Borders

Selecting borders for French braid quilts is no different from doing so for any other style of quilt. If you have used center separators and love the fabric, try it as an outer border; outline separators and accents can also double as inner borders. If you have been unsuccessful at incorporating your inspiration fabric, try it as a border; you may get to use it after all.

Braid Construction

The braids in French braid quilts consist of four basic components. All braids include the braid run, accents, and ending triangles, and these pieces are always cut and sewn in the same way. Basic braids, constructed by starting at one end and continuing to the other, also include starting triangles, whereas center-out braids, in which construction starts at the center and progresses out in both directions, start with center squares. The braid run usually consists of 10 to 12 fabrics, and a single basic braid with a 10-fabric run will finish about 62″ long by 11″ wide. Every segment you add to the braid will add almost 3″ in length, and a center square will add about 5½″. The Anatomy of a French Braid Quilt (page 6) will give you a better understanding of the various parts.

Cutting

The fabrics for the braid run and accents require 40″ of usable width (20″ from the selvage to the center for fat quarters). You can make a 4-braid basic or center-out quilt from ¼ yard of each of the braid-run fabrics, but you will not have enough extra for swatching. Check the cutting instructions that follow to determine whether to purchase extra fabric. Also, although these instructions for a basic braid are common to many projects, sizes do vary from quilt to quilt; be sure to check the fabric requirements for your particular project.

Cutting for the Braid Run

1. For straight ¼ yards, cut 1 strip 8½″ × width of fabric from each braid-run fabric. Then cut each 8½″ × 40+″ piece lengthwise down the center—where the fabric was folded when on the bolt—to obtain 2 pieces, each 8½″ × 20+″. For fat quarters, cut 2 strips 8½″ × width of fabric from each braid-run fabric, being sure to cut crosswise (at right angles to the selvage).

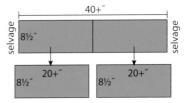

Cutting straight ¼ yards

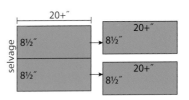

Cutting fat quarters

2. Make 2 piles of fabric, each with an 8½" × 20+" piece of each braid-run fabric. The 2 piles will be used differently.

3. Set aside one of the piles. From the remaining pile, cut 2 segments 2½" wide from each fabric. You may wish to stack the pieces in the order in which you expect them to appear in the braid run and cut several at once. Set all of the braid-run fabric aside, continuing to keep the 2 piles from Step 2 separate.

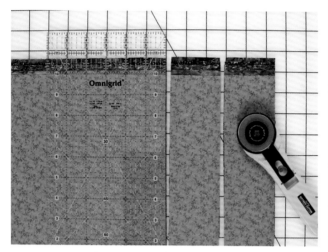

Cut 2 segments from each fabric.

Cutting the Accent Fabric

1. Cut strips 2½" × width of fabric (40+"). You need half as many strips as you have fabrics in the braid run (5 strips for 10 fabrics, 6 for 11 or 12 fabrics). For fat quarters, cut the same number of strips as the number of braid-run fabrics, each 2½" × width of fabric.

2. Cut each full-width strip in half to obtain 2 pieces, each 2½" × 20+".

3. Place all the accent strips with the *uncut* pile of braid-run fabrics.

French Braid Obsession

Cutting Starting Triangles or Center Squares

There are several ways to cut *starting triangles*, depending on the configuration of the piece and the type of print you have selected. For a nondirectional fat quarter, cut a 13″ × 13″ square; then subcut the square twice diagonally to obtain 4 quarter-square triangles.

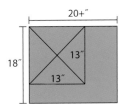

Starting triangles from fat quarter

For directional fabrics, you must use a straight quarter to ensure that all the motifs are oriented in the same direction (all horizontal or all vertical). This cutting configuration may also be used for nondirectional straight quarters. Cut a strip 6½″ × the width of the fabric; then use the 45°-angle line on your ruler or a 45°-45°-90° triangle ruler to cut 4 triangles.

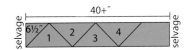

Starting triangles from straight ¼ yard

For one-way prints, in which the print points in one direction, starting triangles must be cut from 2 strips 6½″ wide. Buy ½ yard and use a 45°-45°-90° triangle ruler or the 45°-angle line on your ruler to cut all the triangles in the same direction. If you wish to fussy cut, unroll the fabric from the bolt to count the available motifs and use an Omnigrid 98L ruler as a cutting template.

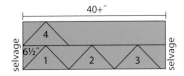

Starting triangles from one-way print

For *center squares*, cut 4 squares 8¼″ × 8¼″ from either a straight or a fat quarter. If you like fussy cutting, this is a good place to indulge, because the squares will march across the center of the finished quilt. Remember that if the fabric is obviously directional and you want the motif to appear vertically in the quilt, you must purchase extra fabric to cut the squares on the bias.

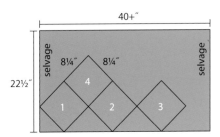

Center squares from directional fabric

Laying Out the Braid

First the good news: Even if your braid run isn't perfect, the eye will try to perceive it as a progression. The bad news: Your eye can only help so much, so it's still best to aim for as smooth a braid run as possible. Fabric looks amazingly different when cut up than when viewed at about the same width on the edge of a bolt. Therefore, although most quilters will balk at this step, it is very important to lay out one entire braid run to see if it flows well.

1. Place a starting triangle on the table, with the longest side toward you. Then lay out a couple of your cut accent strips end to end, so that they extend upward from the point of the triangle. Using the 2 segments that you cut from the braid fabrics, lay out a braid run, leaving spaces at the center to let the accent fabric show through. You may also audition your ending triangle fabric, if you have chosen one. If not, ignore it until you have sewn the braids.

Lay out braid run.

2. Stand back and examine the braid run carefully. If you are not happy with it, try to pinpoint the cause.

- Does one fabric jump out? If so, why? Is it too dark or light? Is it too bright or dull? Try using the wrong side of the fabric, as it is sometimes a shade lighter or grayer.

- Is there too big a jump between two fabrics? If so, try to find another to intersperse between them.

- Do parts of the braid appear to be splotchy? Check to see whether the splotches appear occasionally or throughout a print. If they appear regularly and they bother you, eliminate the fabric; if they seem to occur randomly, as with a hand-dyed fabric, cut two more pieces and look again—sometimes a few irregularities add interest.

- Is the order of the fabrics incorrect? Rearrange one side of the braid to compare with the unaltered side. If you can't cure a perceived defect, try dispensing with a questionable fabric to see if there's an improvement.

3. Each fabric you eliminate will shorten the braid by almost 6″ (assuming there are 2 segments of it in each braid); if you must replace the length that you've lost, adding another fabric to either end of the run is usually the easiest solution. If you really can't decide on the correct order for 2 or 3 fabrics, it may not matter—just pick the order you think works best with the adjacent fabrics.

4. When you are satisfied with the braid run, return the cut segments to their pile and cut 6 more 2½″ segments from each fabric in the same pile. If you have replaced a fabric, cut a new 8½″ strip; from that strip, cut 8 segments 2½″ wide and use those in place of the ones you discarded.

Cutting the Ending Triangles

Even if you believe that you have the perfect fabric for the ending triangles, cut it later. At best, you won't use them until the braids are finished; why have all those bias edges sitting around stretching? Once the braids are finished, cut either 4 squares 7″ × 7″ from a straight or a fat quarter for *basic braids* or 8 squares 7″ × 7″ from a half yard or 2 fat quarters for *center-out braids*. Each square will be cut in half diagonally to yield either 8 half-square triangles for basic braids or 16 for center-out braids.

Cut ending triangles.

Sewing

Use a consistent ¼˝ seam allowance.

Sewing Accent to Braid Fabrics

1. Sew a half strip of accent fabric to each 8½˝ × 20+˝ strip in the uncut pile of braid-run fabrics; match the long edges. Press all seams toward the braid fabric (the larger piece).

2. Subcut each seamed pair into 8 segments 2½˝ × 10½˝ each.

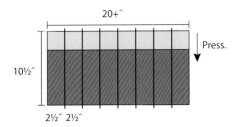

Subcut braid segments.

Sewing Braids

> ## Note
>
> To ensure that both sides of your braid are approximately the same length when you finish, always sew with the piece you are adding on top.

BASIC BRAIDS

1. Lay out a starting triangle right side up, with the long side closest to you.

2. Place an unaccented 2½˝ × 8½˝ segment of the first braid-run fabric right side down on the left side of the triangle, matching the 90° angle at the top of the triangle. The side of the triangle is longer than the segment. Pin if you like, rotate the triangle, and sew toward the 90° angle, keeping the braid segment on top.

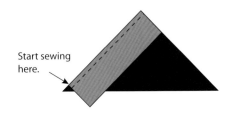

Sew first braid segment.

3. Sew the first unaccented braid fabric to each of the other starting triangles by chain piecing.

4. Press the seam toward the newly attached braid segment. All pressing will be done in this manner *with one exception:* If you are certain that you will not be adding separators to the quilt, it is permissible to press the seams in 2 of the braids in this manner and the seams in the other 2 braids toward the previous segment. The 2 braids with seams pressed toward the previous segments will not lie as flat as the others, but this will make it easier to sew the braids together later because the seams will nest together.

5. With the longest side of the starting triangle closest to you, place an accented 2½˝ × 10½˝ segment of the first braid fabric on the right edge of the triangle, with right sides together. The top 90° angles and the seamlines should match, and the seam allowances should be facing opposite directions. If you cannot match both the top edges and the seamlines, match only the seamlines.

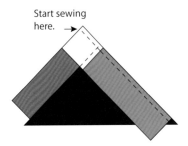

Sew second braid segment.

> ## Note
>
> If you have pressed two of your braids in opposite directions, as in Step 4, re-press the seam between the braid segment and the accent fabric as necessary so that the seams butt.

6. Repeat Step 5 for the other triangles and press the seams as you did in Step 4.

7. Add the remaining braid segments in the same manner, alternating the plain and accented segments of each braid fabric on opposite sides of the braid.

8. When you have finished a series of braid segments, start with the first braid-run fabric again and repeat the sequence. When you are done, you will not have any segments left. If you prefer, you may reverse the braid segment sequence rather than repeat it, as was done in *Boston Braid* (page 56). If you choose this option, do not reuse the

Braid Construction ◆ ◆ 19 ◆

last braid fabric at the center of the braid. Instead, you will have 4 plain and 4 accented segments of that fabric left, and your quilt will be approximately 3″ shorter.

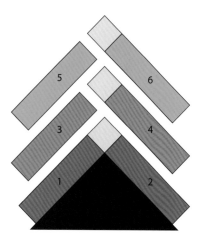

Piecing sequence

9. Select and cut the ending triangles (refer to Cutting the Ending Triangles, page 18).

10. Pick up an ending triangle and, with right sides together, align the long side of the triangle with the left side of the top of the braid strip. Approximately ¾″ of the triangle should hang off the top of the braid, and the 90° angle of the triangle should point to the second seam from the top on the opposite side of the braid. Pin along the edges of the triangle. The braid segment will be longer than the triangle. Don't worry; everything will be adjusted later. (If the size of the braid changes, the positioning of the 90° angle will also change. Just leave the ¾″ tip of the triangle at the top of the braid, and it will work.)

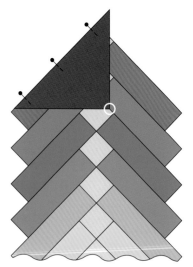

Alignment for ending triangle

11. Flip over the entire unit and sew with the triangle on the bottom to avoid stretching the bias. Repeat for the other braids and press as before. Then repeat with the remaining triangles on the top right sides of the braids.

CENTER-OUT BRAIDS

The construction of center-out braids is virtually identical to that of basic braids with the following exceptions.

1. Start with a center square and add unaccented segments to 2 opposite sides, matching the ends of the segments to the top and bottom of the center square as shown. Sew 2 braid segments to each of the other squares by chain piecing. Press toward the braid segments. If your center squares are cut from directional fabric and you want the print to face the same way in all the braids, you must orient them all in the same direction when attaching the first set of segments.

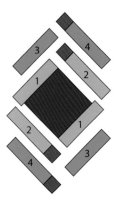

Piecing sequence for center-out braids

2. Continue building from the center out in both directions. The sewing sequence is the same as before (Steps 4–7, page 19), but when the braids are complete, you will have an entire braid sequence on each of 2 opposite sides of the center square.

3. Add ending triangles to both ends of each braid (Steps 10 and 11, above).

Trimming or Marking the Braids

You now have braids with zigzag edges; no matter how you have decided to join them, you will need a straight edge. If you plan to sew the braids directly to each other (*Flashback*, page 28), you will trim off the dog ears now; if you intend to add separators (*Garden in Need of Weeding*, page 31), you will mark a cutting line now for later trimming. In either case, you will need a gridded cutting mat at least 24″ long (longer is better), a ruler at least 6″ × 24″ (wider is okay), and either a rotary cutter for trimming or a pencil for marking. I prefer a graphite mechanical pencil for marking, because the line is thin and permanent and the point stays sharp. If you can't see graphite on dark fabrics, use a lighter color for those sections.

Pressing

Using a side-to-side motion, press the braids, right side up, beginning at the starting triangle and working toward the top. If you have pressed the seams in 2 braids in the opposite direction (as in Step 4, page 19), press those braids in a similar manner, but start from the ending triangle. Press center-out braids from the center square toward the ends. The goal is to eliminate any pleats in the seamlines, while also avoiding possible stretching that can occur when the braids are pressed along their length.

Trimming for Basic Braids without Separators

1. Although there are no bias edges, the entire braid is on the bias and will easily flex crosswise. Lay out a braid right side up on the cutting mat, smoothing it as flat as possible without stretching it lengthwise. If you do not have enough space to spread the braid full length, accordion fold it at the starting triangle end and begin with the ending triangle. Without letting either end dangle from the edge of the cutting surface, align the outside points of the nearest zigzag edge with a line on the cutting mat.

Align zigzag edge with line on mat.

2. Determine your cutting width by measuring out from a centermost accent corner to the innermost corner of the zigzag edge. Measure all braids in several places and in both directions from the center—the measurements may vary. Use the smallest number—usually from 5½″ to 5¾″, depending on your seam allowances—as the measurement for trimming the sides of your braids.

Measure from center out.

3. Keeping the outer points of one side of the braid aligned with a mat line, place a long line on your 24″ ruler on the centermost corners of the accent squares. (To obtain the 5½″ to 5¾″ measurement you need, you will usually use the ¼″, ⅜″, or ½″ line on a 6″-wide ruler.)

Align ruler for cutting or marking.

TIP

If you find that a few of the center corners don't line up with your ruler, check whether you have cut an accent rectangle instead of a square. Look carefully and measure to make sure; rip out and replace any segment that is the wrong size. If you are careful, you can do this without removing the subsequent segments. If you find that all your accents are squares and the corners are only slightly out of alignment, leave the braid as it is. If you have cut and sewn correctly and a few corners are moderately out of alignment, you can pull the braid gently to realign the corners. Do not pull on the side of the braid directly adjacent to the nonaligned corner; instead, walk your fingers down the seam that attaches the misaligned accent square to its neighbor and pull gently on the end of it. If, after you let go, the braid pops back to its original position, leave it as it is. If the braid is severely out of alignment, make an executive decision whether to leave it as is or sew another braid.

Adjust misaligned accent square.

4. Once your braid is properly aligned along the 24″ length of your ruler, use a rotary cutter to trim the edge. Cut only approximately 12″–18″ at a time—no matter how careful you have been, the braid does not always lie perfectly straight. Without moving the braid, place the ruler on the opposite edge, realign it with the center squares, and trim.

Trim braid.

5. Before moving this top section of the braid, trim the ending triangles. Use a ruler at least 12″ long and align a set of crosswise ruler lines with each edge you just trimmed. The ¼″ ruler line must meet the top point of the top accent square at the top of the braid. Recheck to make sure that your ¼″ line is at the top point and that your cutting edge is at a true right angle to the sides of the braid. Then use your rotary cutter to trim across the top of the braid.

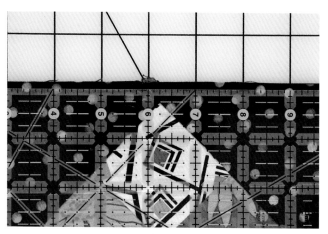

Trim ending triangles.

6. Work your way down the braid, measuring and trimming as many times as necessary. If you have been unable to lay out the entire strip at once, roll up the top trimmed end and unfold the bottom untrimmed portion as you go. Remember that once you have trimmed the edges, they are on the bias, so do not let the end of the braid dangle from the edge of the table. If you reposition the braid and the end of the ruler does not meet your cut edge, move the ruler back up the trimmed portion of the braid until it does. Begin your new cut there (Step 1, at the right).

7. After you trim the sides of the braid strip, trim the starting triangles. Trim from the point where your cut edge intersects the seam between the first braid segment and the starting triangle across to the corresponding point on the opposite side of the braid.

Note

This line is not always parallel to the bottom edge of your starting triangle.

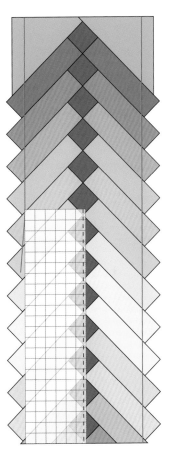

Trim starting triangles.

8. After you trim an entire strip, gently carry it to the sewing machine and staystitch the bias sides within the seam allowances—approximately ⅛″ from each long edge. Trim the other strips similarly, staystitching each braid immediately after cutting.

Marking for Basic Braids with Separators

1. Press, align, and measure the braids as in Trimming for Basic Braids without Separators (Steps 1–3, page 21). Instead of cutting as in Step 4 (page 22), draw a pencil line on each side. Because the fabric shifts easily, mark with short overlapping pencil strokes while using your "off" hand to hold the ruler. As you move the pencil down the length of the braid, move the other hand along with it, so that the hand on the ruler is always pressing beside your pencil, keeping the fabric stationary where you are marking. If when you reposition the ruler you find that the end does not meet the end of your drawn line, slide the ruler back up the marked portion of the braid until it does; begin your new line there. Mark both edges of the braid before moving or refolding it.

Reposition end of ruler to meet the straight line.

2. Trim the ending and starting triangles as in Trimming for Basic Braids (Steps 5 and 7, pages 22 and at the left), using the drawn line, rather than the cut edge, as a reference point.

3. If you know that you will be adding separators, measure the length of each braid down the center while you have it on the table (see Determining the Separator Length, page 25).

Trimming and Marking for Center-Out Braids

Measure the braid width across the center square, adding ¼″ beyond each point to allow for the seam allowances. Use the method for marking basic braids (Steps 1–3, page 23) to trim or mark the sides of the center-out braids. The marked line (or cut) must be ¼″ outside the outer corners of the center square to allow for seam allowances. Finish with or without separators.

Line marked on center-out braid

Sewing Braids Together

If you have decided not to add separators, you are ready to sew the braids together.

1. If you have pressed the seams in one direction for 2 braids and in the opposite direction for the other 2, take one of each type of braid. Lay a braid in which you have pressed the seams toward the starting triangle face up on a table. Lay a braid in which you have pressed the seams toward the ending triangles face down on top of the first fabric, butting all seams at the right edge and matching both ends. Pin each seam. Repeat for the second set of braids, replicating the placement and sewing on the same edge each time. If you are sewing center-out braids, pay particular attention to the corners where the center squares meet—a misalignment there is very obvious.

2. Start at an ending triangle end and sew a pair of braids using a medium or slow speed—the presser foot tends to jump when it crosses the diagonal seamlines. Press the long seams open. Repeat for the second braid pair.

3. Sew the larger units from Step 2 together and press the seam open. You may now finish your top by adding borders, referring to page 8 if necessary.

Adding Separators

The optional addition of separators depends on the individual quilter and the requirements of the project. However, before you can add any separators, you must determine both their length and their width. If possible, cut separators on the lengthwise grain, because the bias braids benefit from this added stability. If you do not want to purchase fabric for the entire length, buy enough for half the length and piece it together. It is permissible to cut crosswise if absolutely necessary to take advantage of a design element, as when using a directional fabric.

Separator Width and Length

Separator width is purely subjective. For a basic braid, I often cut a 2½″ center strip and two 1½″ outline strips, for a total finished width of 4″. If you make a larger quilt or want to take advantage of a particular motif, you can use larger separators, but make sure they don't overwhelm the braids.

DETERMINING THE SEPARATOR LENGTH

1. To measure the length of each braid down the center, if necessary fold the braid in half, with wrong sides together. Double the measurement to obtain the braid's full length. Always include the seam allowances in this measurement. Measure and write down the length of each braid, because they are often different. If there is a difference of more than 1″, examine the offending braid(s) to see if you have inadvertently omitted one set of segments. If so, go back and insert them.

TIP

It is not unusual to fold the braid and find that the two ends cannot be matched because the angles are different. If this occurs, match the vertical centers—that is, the tip of the top accent square with the horizontal center of the starting triangle for the basic braid or the tips of the top accent squares on both ends for the center-out style.

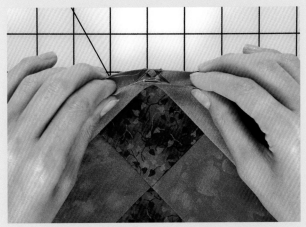

Match ends of braids at centers to measure length.

---

2. Examine the numbers you have written and pick a number that is near the average. This will be the length that you will cut your separators.

3. While the braids are still folded, finger-press a center crease on the marked vertical lines at the edges of each braid. When you open the braid, make a horizontal mark in the seam allowance at each crease. You will use these marks later when you are attaching the separators. These marks may not all fall at exactly the same point in the braid run on each braid or even on the 2 sides of each braid. You will compensate for this later.

Constructing Two-Fabric Separators

1. Cut enough 1½″ strips for your outline strips. For a basic or center-out (4-braid) quilt, this will be either 6 strips if you purchased fabric for the full length or 12 if you purchased fabric for half the length or have decided to cut the strips crosswise on your fabric.

2. Cut enough 2½″ strips for the center strips—3 if you purchased fabric for the full length or 6 if you either purchased fabric for half the length or have decided to cut crosswise.

3. If necessary, sew the outline strips end to end into 2 long outline strips of equal length for each separator. Press the seams open. Again, if necessary, sew the center strips end to end into a long center strip. Press the seam open.

4. Sew an outline strip to each side of each center strip. If one fabric has been cut crosswise and the other lengthwise, place the lengthwise-grain fabric on top as you send it through the machine. Press the seams in either direction and trim the separators to the desired length, making sure that all lengths are the same and that they all match the number you have chosen.

Sewing the Separators to the Braids

1. Find the marks that you made at the approximate centers of the braid strips when you measured their lengths. These marks probably do not all fall at the same place on all braids. Select a spot in the braid run that is close to all 8 marked "centers" and use that same spot as the center on all 4 braids to ensure that the segments align across the quilt's width. Use a different color of pencil (or pins) to mark your new "universal center."

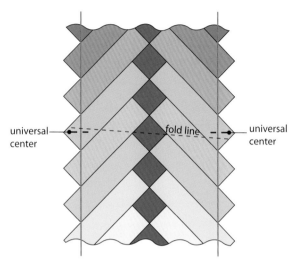

Marks may not fall at same center point on both sides. Select common point and mark it as your universal center.

2. Keeping the separator band on top, pin the ends and the center of the separator to the ends and universal center mark on a braid strip. Lay out the entire unit on a table and gently adjust the braid strip to the separator, matching the long raw edge of the separator band to the pencil line on the braid strip. If you must ease or stretch the braid to make it fit, measure again to make sure that you have cut your separator bands to the correct length and marked all halves correctly. Pin at every braid seam.

Pin separator band to braid strip.

3. Attach a ¼" seam presser foot to your sewing machine. Use the raw edge of the separator as your guide as you sew the band to the braid strip, keeping the separator on top. Sew at a slow to moderate speed for best results.

4. Take the unpressed unit back to your cutting mat. Using the same raw edge of the separator as a guide, trim the zigzag edges off that side of the braid strip with your ruler and rotary cutter. Press the seam toward the separator.

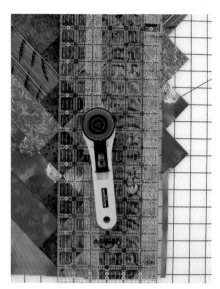

Trim zigzag edge even with edge of separator.

5. Repeat Steps 1–4 twice more, so you end up with 3 braid strips, each with a separator band attached to the same (left or right) side.

6. Sew 2 of the units from Step 5 to each other and the third to the unattached braid strip, using the same methods of matching, pinning, and pressing.

7. Purchase everything you need to complete your quilt: fabric for borders, backing, and binding; quilting thread; and batting. Sew the lengthwise inner borders to your 2 zigzag outer edges in the same way that you attached the separators, using the same lengthwise measurement as you did for the separator bands. (If you use stacked borders, page 8, you may add the crosswise border first, so the lengthwise border measurement will change.) Add the remaining borders and finish the quilt.

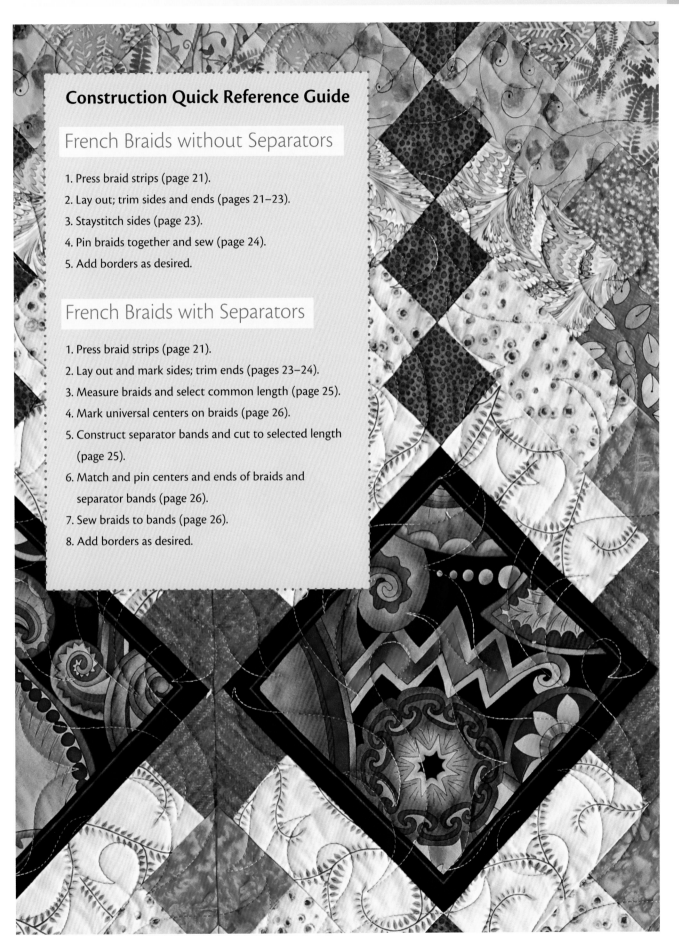

Construction Quick Reference Guide

French Braids without Separators

1. Press braid strips (page 21).
2. Lay out; trim sides and ends (pages 21–23).
3. Staystitch sides (page 23).
4. Pin braids together and sew (page 24).
5. Add borders as desired.

French Braids with Separators

1. Press braid strips (page 21).
2. Lay out and mark sides; trim ends (pages 23–24).
3. Measure braids and select common length (page 25).
4. Mark universal centers on braids (page 26).
5. Construct separator bands and cut to selected length (page 25).
6. Match and pin centers and ends of braids and separator bands (page 26).
7. Sew braids to bands (page 26).
8. Add borders as desired.

Flashback

Flashback by Patricia E. Ritter, 55½" × 90½"

Bloomin' Braid Runner
by Jane Hardy Miller, 11″ × 60″

 Fabric Requirements

Note

This center-out French braid quilt may be made using only ¼ yard of each braid fabric rather than the ½ yard listed. This assumes that every fabric has at least 40″ of *usable* width and that you will make *no* errors in cutting; therefore, I recommend that you purchase ½ yard. However, if there is only ¼ yard (fat or not) of one of your fabrics, buy it and cut carefully.

Purchase Now

½ yard *each* of 12 fabrics for braid run—fat quarters okay

½ yard for accent squares—2 fat quarters okay

¼ yard for center squares—fat quarter okay

Purchase Later

½ yard nondirectional print for ending triangles—2 fat quarters okay

½ yard for inner borders

2⅜ yards for outer borders (includes extra for appliqué cutouts)

½ yard for leaf cutouts (purchase more fabric if the leaf motifs are scattered far apart in your fabric print)

⅜ yard green for stems

5½ yards for backing, pieced lengthwise

⅝ yard for binding

60″ × 95″ batting

Cutting

Refer to pages 15–18 for basic cutting instructions.

BRAIDS: From each fabric, cut 1 strip 8½″ × width of fabric; then cut the strips in half. *Or* from each fat quarter, cut 2 strips 8½″ wide from selvage to center.

ACCENTS: Cut 6 strips 2½″ × width of fabric; cut in half at the center fold. *Or* from fat quarters, cut 12 strips 2½″ wide from selvage to center.

CENTER SQUARES: Cut 4 squares 8¼″ × 8¼″.

ENDING TRIANGLES: Cut 8 squares 7″ × 7″; then cut in half diagonally to obtain 16 half-square triangles.

INNER BORDERS: Cut 7 strips 1¾″ × width of fabric.

OUTER BORDERS: Cut 4 strips 5″ × length of fabric.

 Construction

Refer to pages 19–26 for basic instructions.

1. Separate the braid fabrics into 2 piles.

2. From the first pile, cut 2 segments 2½″ × 8½″ from each fabric. Audition with accent and triangle fabrics and rearrange or replace as needed. Cut 6 more segments from every fabric in that pile (pages 17–18).

3. Sew an accent strip to each fabric in the second pile of braid fabrics (page 19). Subcut each into 8 segments 2½″ × 10½″.

4. Construct 4 center-out braids (page 20), using the pressing alternative on page 21.

5. Trim and staystitch the braids (pages 21–25).

6. Sew the braids together (page 24).

7. Construct and attach borders (pages 8–9).

8. Audition fabric for appliqué pieces, using cutouts from the border, from another fabric, or a combination of the 2, as in the main photo. To make a border flower appear to encroach into the center of the quilt, cut a matching flower from the leftover border fabric and sew the corresponding part of it into the seam adjacent to the partial flower in the border—the 2 pieces will appear to be an entire flower. You may also construct your own flowers and leaves, as in *Braid in Bloom*.

9. Make stems from bias strips. For ½″ finished stems, cut the strips slightly less than 1″ wide and use a bias tape maker to create the finished edges you need in order to appliqué. Or, you can cut the strips slightly more than 1″ wide, fold them in half and sew a seam down the length of the bias using an ⅛″ seam allowance. Then, fold the seam to the center back of the stem and press. Or, use another method of your choice.

10. Appliqué pieces to the top, using your favorite method (pages 7–8).

11. Layer the top with the batting and backing, quilt, and bind.

Braid in Bloom by Jane Hardy Miller, 52″ × 71″. Some appliqué shapes were drawn freehand; some were made using June Tailor templates.

Garden in Need of Weeding

Garden in Need of Weeding by Jane Hardy Miller, 53½″ × 74″

◆ Fabric Requirements

Note

This French braid variation requires 1 yard of ombré fabric for *each* braid. However, there is plenty of fabric within that yard to make each braid much longer (up to 101″) if you use more of the width.

If you decide to select your own braid run, you will need a minimum of ¼ yard each of 9 fabrics for the braid run (see Note, page 29). Follow the directions for a center-out braid with separators (pages 20 and 24).

Purchase Now

3¼ yards ombré fabric for the braid run

⅝ yard for accent squares

¼ yard for center squares—fat quarter okay

Purchase Later

½ yard nondirectional print for ending triangles— fat quarters okay

1⅞ yards for separator center strips (1 yard if you prefer to piece the strips)

1 yard for separator outline strips

⅜ yard for inner borders

1⅞ yards for outer borders

3⅜ yards for backing, pieced crosswise (4½ yards if pieced lengthwise)

½ yard for binding

58″ × 78″ batting

◆ Cutting

Refer to pages 15–18 for basic instructions. Read Prepare Ombré Fabric (at the right) before cutting.

BRAIDS: Cut 12 strips 8½″ × width of fabric.

ACCENTS: Cut 6 strips 2½″ × width of fabric.

CENTER SQUARES: Cut 3 squares 8¼″ × 8¼″.

ENDING TRIANGLES: Cut 6 squares 7″ × 7″; then cut the squares in half diagonally to obtain 12 half-square triangles.

SEPARATOR CENTER STRIPS: Cut 2 strips 2¾″ × length of fabric. *Or* cut 4 strips 2¾″ × length of fabric if you prefer to piece the separators end to end.

SEPARATOR OUTLINE STRIPS: Cut 8 strips 1½″ × length of fabric.

INNER BORDERS: Cut 6 strips 1½″ × width of fabric.

OUTER BORDERS: Cut 4 strips 5½″ × length of fabric.

◆ Construction

Prepare Ombré Fabric

Ombré fabrics have colors that gradually shade from one to another across the width of the fabric, creating the illusion of stripes along the length of the piece. There are several types of ombré fabric; examine yours to see which you have, as it may make a difference in the way you cut.

Some ombré fabrics have two color runs across the width of the fabric. One type starts a sequence at the selvage, changes color or value up to the center fold, then repeats the sequence. Another type begins a sequence at the selvage, changes color or value up to the center fold, then reverses the original sequence. A third type of ombré starts with one color at the selvage and changes color (or value) across the entire width of the fabric. For results similar to those in the photo quilt, the first type of fabric should be used, although the other types will also create interesting effects.

Types of ombré fabric

1. Examine your fabric. Depending on the type you have, you may be able to cut 24″ of continuous width from each 8½″ × 40+″ braid strip, as was done for the quilt in the main photo. One end of the 24″ section will appear as fabric 1 next to the center square; the other end will become fabric 9 and will end the braid and sit next to the ending triangles. Decide which 24″ color sequence you like and cut that same section from each of the 12 strips. (You may save fabric if you cut off the 24″ piece before you cut the 8½″ strips.)

2. Stack the excised sections in front of you. Place a 24″ section on the table in front of you, with the "center" end closest to you. Place another section next to it, so that it is a mirror image of the first. If you look at the sections, the colors should match all the way from the bottom to the top of both (refer to the photo below). Pay attention, because it is easy to reverse a section. Continue stacking pairs of
sections and checking them against each other until you have 2 piles, each with 6 sections 8½″ × 24″.

You will not be able use a continuous 24″ section of some ombré fabrics, because there won't be enough contrast in what would be 2 adjacent segments to make a visual difference. In that case, leave the strips the full width of the fabric and orient them as above. You will decide later exactly where to cut to adjust for the lack of contrast.

Construction

Refer to pages 15–24 for basic instructions.

1. Select the right-hand pile of ombré sections and sew an accent strip to the left edge of each section. Press. If you have precut a 24″ continuous section of ombré fabric, cut down the accent strips to just over 24″ before sewing. If you have left the ombré sections the full width, sew an accent strip to the entire piece.

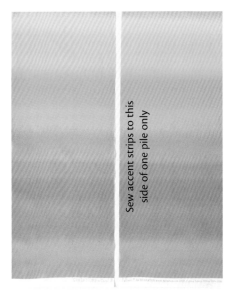

Sew accent strips to this side of one pile only

Orient strips as mirror images.

2. From each accented strip from Step 1, cut 9 segments 2½″ wide (page 19). You will be using only 22½″ of the 24″ strip, so be careful to cut the same color sections from each piece; it may help to stack them carefully before cutting. If you are using the entire width of the fabric, examine the strip carefully and decide where across the width you will cut your 9 segments. You will probably cut a few segments from near a selvage, then skip a section, cut a few more segments, skip another section, and so on until you end up near the opposite selvage. Cut every 8½″ strip identically.

3. From the remaining, unaccented pile, cut 9 segments 2½″ wide, being careful to cut sections that are identical to each other and to those in Step 2.

4. Construct 3 braids using the center-out method (page 20). Be careful to orient each unaccented segment so that it is a mirror image of its corresponding accented segment.

5. Mark the sides, trim the ends, and measure the braid lengths (pages 23–25).

6. Sew the outline and center separator strips into 2 separator bands (page 25).

7. Sew the separator bands to 2 braid strips (page 26).

8. Sew the braid/separator units together (page 26).

9. Construct and attach borders (pages 8–9).

10. Layer the top with the batting and backing, quilt, and bind.

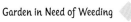

What Was I Thinking? by Patricia E. Ritter, 65½″ × 83¾″

Although its appearance may fool you, this quilt is a center-out braid. Patricia pieced the braid-run fabrics with background fabrics in varying proportions to achieve the dramatic effect.

As with any French braid quilt, the fabric selection is the biggest challenge. Select the braid run as for any braid: run, accent, center square. Then choose a color for the background and select several fabrics similar in color, value, and intensity to use as the background between the braids. Patricia used 6 turquoise fabrics, and the instructions are designed to reflect this; however, 5, 4, or even 3 could be used with adjustments for yardage.

Braid-run fabrics are numbered as usual, 1 through 11 from the center out. Background fabrics are labeled A through F from the center out.

Fabric Requirements

Purchase Now

⅜ yard each of fabrics 1–8 of the braid run

¼ yard each of fabrics 9–11 of the braid run

¼ yard of fabric A of background fabrics

⅝ yard each of fabrics B–F of background fabrics

1 yard for accent squares and border cornerstones

Either 5 preprinted, prebordered 8¼″ × 8¼″ squares

or ¼ yard center square fabric and ⅓ yard center square border fabric

Purchase Later

½ yard for ending triangles

½ yard for inner borders

2¼ yards for outer borders cut lengthwise (1⅛ yards if you prefer to piece the strips)

5 yards for backing, pieced lengthwise

⅝ yard for binding

70″ × 88″ batting

Cutting

Refer to pages 15–18 for basic instructions.

Note

Labeling the braid and background strips with the correct number or letter and size will help as you sew everything together.

BRAIDS: Cut 2 strips the width of the fabric by the following measurements:

Fabric 1: 5¾″
Fabric 2: 5½″
Fabric 3: 5¼″
Fabric 4: 5″
Fabric 5: 4¾″
Fabric 6: 4½″
Fabric 7: 4¼″
Fabric 8: 4″
Fabric 9: 3¾″
Fabric 10: 3½″
Fabric 11: 3¼″

BACKGROUND: Cut strips the width of the fabric by the following measurements:

Fabric A: 2 strips 3¼″
Fabric B: 2 strips 3½″ and 2 strips 4¾″
Fabric C: 2 strips 3¾″ and 2 strips 5″
Fabric D: 2 strips 4″ and 2 strips 5¼″
Fabric E: 2 strips 4¼″ and 2 strips 5¾″
Fabric F: 2 strips 4½″ and 2 strips 5½″

ACCENT: Cut 11 strips 2½″ × width of fabric. Cut 1 strip 4½″ × width of fabric; then subcut into 4 squares 4½″ × 4½″.

EITHER PREPRINTED CENTER SQUARES: Cut 5 squares 8¼″ × 8¼″.

OR NONPREPRINTED CENTER SQUARES AND CENTER BORDERS: For the center squares, cut 5 squares 7¼″ × 7¼″ for the squares. For the center borders, cut 1 strip 8¼″ × width of fabric; then subcut into 10 segments 1″ × 8¼″. Cut the remainder of the strip down to 7¼″ and subcut into 10 segments 1″ × 7¼″.

ENDING TRIANGLES: Cut 10 squares 7″ × 7″; then cut in half diagonally to obtain 20 half-square triangles.

INNER BORDER: Cut 7 strips 1¾″ × width of fabric.

OUTER BORDER: Cut 4 strips 4½″ × length of fabric. *Or,* if you prefer to piece lengthwise, cut 7 strips 4½″ × length of fabric.

◆ Construction

Refer to pages 19–26 for basic instructions.

1. If using nonpreprinted fabric for center squares, sew 1″ × 7¼″ pieces of center border fabric to opposite sides of each center square. Press toward the border. Sew 1″ × 8¼″ pieces of center border fabric to the remaining 2 sides of each center square. Press toward the border. These are your center squares.

2. Cut fabrics 1–11, A–F, and the accent strips to 28″ in width. You will not use the excess. Divide the strips into 2 piles: In the first pile, place 1 strip each of fabrics 1–11 and 1 strip of fabric A. Add 1 strip of *each width* of fabrics B–F and all the accent strips to the same pile. Set aside until Step 5.

3. From the remaining strips of fabrics 1–11 and A–F, sew the following pairs, matching long edges. Press the seams toward the braid-run fabrics.

Fabrics 1 and A (3¼″)	Fabrics 7 and B (4¾″)
Fabrics 2 and B (3½″)	Fabrics 8 and C (5″)
Fabrics 3 and C (3¾″)	Fabrics 9 and D (5¼″)
Fabrics 4 and D (4″)	Fabrics 10 and F (5½″)
Fabrics 5 and E (4¼″)	Fabrics 11 and E (5¾″)
Fabrics 6 and F (4½″)	

4. Cut 2 segments 2½″ wide from each paired set from Step 3 and audition with accent and center square fabrics. If the pairings are satisfactory, cut 8 more segments 2½″ wide from every paired set.

5. Sew together and press the braid-run and background fabric strips from Step 2, pairing them as in Step 3.

6. Sew an accent strip to the braid-run fabric edge of each braid run/background strip set from Step 5. Press the seams toward the braid-run fabric. Cut 10 segments 2½″ wide from each set.

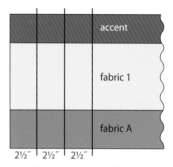

Sew accent to braid strip set.

7. Construct 5 center-out braids (page 20), using the pressing alternative on page 21.

8. Trim and staystitch the braids (pages 21–23).

9. Sew the braids together (page 24).

10. Add borders, using the cornerstone method (page 9).

11. Layer the top with the batting and backing, quilt, and bind.

Tropical Christmas

Tropical Christmas by Jane Hardy Miller, 54″ in diameter

This skirt is made from 10 basic braids that diminish in width from bottom to top. They are then trimmed into tall triangles and sewn together. It could also work as a table topper if the last seam were sewn shut and a circle appliquéd over the center opening. See Robin Fouquette's more traditional tree skirt, the inspiration for this version, on page 41.

Note

To achieve the look of multiple concentric stars, there must be contrast between some of the braid-run fabrics. Thus, the usual rules of French braid fabric selection do not apply.

 # Fabric Requirements

⅜ yard or 2 fat quarters each of fabrics 1–4 and fabric 7 of the braid run

¼ yard each of fabrics 5 and 6 of the braid run—fat quarters okay

¼ yard for accent squares—fat quarter okay

1¼ yards nondirectional or directional print for starting triangles (1½ yards if using a one-way print) (The triangles in the project tree skirt were fussy cut from approximately 2½ yards of fabric, but the amount needed will vary with the motif. These are large triangles, so buy plenty of fabric if you intend to fussy cut.)

4¼ yards freezer paper (at least 18″ wide)

3⅜ yards for back

½ yard for binding

58″ × 58″ batting

 # Cutting

Refer to pages 15–18 for basic instructions.

BRAIDS: *EITHER* cut strips the width of the fabric by the following measurements; then cut all the strips of fabrics 1–6 in half to measure 20+″ wide. Do not cut the strips of fabric 7 in half.

Fabrics 1 and 2: 1 strip each 12½″

Fabrics 3 and 4: 1 strip each 10″

Fabrics 5 and 6: 1 strip each 7″

Fabric 7: 1 strip 4″ and 1 strip 6″

OR from fat quarters, cut the following from selvage to center:

Fabrics 1 and 2: 2 strips each 12½″

Fabrics 3 and 4: 2 strips each 10″

Fabrics 5 and 6: 2 strips each 7″

Fabric 7: 2 strips 4″ and 2 strips 6″

ACCENTS: *EITHER* cut 3 strips 2″ × width of fabric and then cut the strips in half, *OR* from a fat quarter, cut 6 strips 2″ wide from selvage to center.

STARTING TRIANGLES: *EITHER* from nondirectional fabric, cut 2 strips 19″ × width of fabric; subcut into 3 squares 19″ × 19″; cut each square twice diagonally to yield 12 quarter-square triangles (you will use 10).

OR from directional fabric, cut 4 strips 9½″ × width of fabric; subcut into 10 triangles, each with a 19″ base.

OR from a one-way print, cut 5 strips 9½″ × width of fabric; subcut into 10 triangles, each with a 19″ base.

OR, to fussy cut, make a triangle template with a 19″ base, and select and mark the triangles on the wrong side of the fabric before cutting, or use a Setting Triangle ruler by Little Foot as a template.

Construction

Refer to pages 19–26 for basic instructions.

1. Separate braid fabrics 1–6 into 2 piles. Set aside braid fabric 7.

2. From the first pile, cut 2 segments 2″ wide from fabrics 1–6 and cut 1 segment 2½″ wide from each size (4″ and 6″) of fabric 7. Audition with accent and triangle fabrics; rearrange or replace as needed. Cut 8 more segments from fabrics 1–6 in the original pile (pages 17–18); then cut 9 more segments from each size strip of fabric 7.

3. Sew an accent strip to each fabric in the second, uncut pile of braid fabrics. Subcut each seamed pair into 10 segments 2″ wide (page 19).

4. If your starting triangles have varying motifs, arrange them in a pleasing circular pattern. Number the triangles from 1 to 10; the skirt opening will be between braids 1 and 10.

5. Construct 10 braids from fabrics 1–6 (pages 19–20), using the pressing alternative on page 21.

6. Add the 4″ segments of fabric 7 to the left tops of the braids, as if they were unaccented braid strips. Press the seams in the same direction as the rest of those in each braid. Add the 6″ segments of fabric 7 to the right tops of the braids, as if they were accented braid strips. Press the seams in the same direction as the rest of each braid.

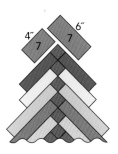

7. Make 5 freezer paper triangles, each with a 17¼″ base. It is sometimes possible to draw one triangle and then iron several layers of freezer paper together and cut as one. Reheat with the iron if they don't want to separate.

a. Draw a 17¼″ line across the freezer paper; mark the center (8⅝″).

b. From that center point, draw a perpendicular line 26½″ long.

c. Connect the ends of the 17¼″ line to the ends of the vertical line.

d. Check the angles with a protractor. The angles on the baseline should be exactly 72°. The angle at the top point of the triangle should be 36°.

e. If you have cut more than one triangle at once, mark the vertical center line on every triangle as in Step 7b.

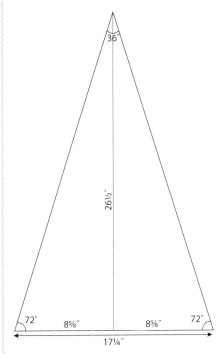

Draw triangle template.

> **Note**
>
> You could also use a template made from acetate to mark sewing lines directly onto the braids themselves, but this is less accurate than the method described.

8. Press braids 1 and 2 (page 21). Place them on a table, right sides together, with braid 2 on top. Match the zigzag edges as well as you can without pinning. If you have pressed correctly, the seams will butt. Feel the top point of the starting triangles and adjust the seams so that they nest together; pin. Do the same for the top accents and for one pair of accents near the center. Turn the pieces over so that braid 1 is on top. Use silk pins, if possible, because the tiny heads will make the piece less lumpy when you turn it over. Larger pins, all placed on the braid 1 side, have been used in the photo for visibility's sake.

9. Pin every zigzag on both edges of the pair, butting the seams. Pin the top point of the braid.

Pin centers and edges together.

10. Press the freezer paper onto braid 1, matching the bottom edge of the starting triangles with the edge of the freezer paper and matching the top point of the braids and the center of the starting triangles with the center line on the paper. The point of the paper will extend past the end of the braid. Pin each seamline close to the point where it intersects the freezer paper.

Press freezer paper onto braid.

11. Sew along an edge of the freezer paper.

12. Trim the braid ¼″ outside the edge of the freezer paper. Unpin everything. Repeat for 4 other pairs, pressing the freezer paper onto the odd-numbered braids and sewing on the same (left or right) edge each time. Do not press the seams yet.

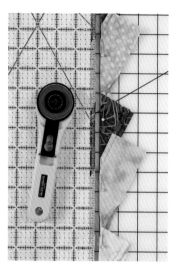

Trim ¼″ from paper edge.

13. Sew 2 pairs into a set of 4, keeping the freezer paper on top. Sew another 2 pairs, adding a third pair. Sew the 2 sections together.

Sew pairs together.

14. At the opening between braids 1 and 10, draw a line at the unseamed edge of the freezer paper on braid 1. Peel off the freezer paper, rewarming it with an iron if necessary, and press it onto braid 10, matching the edges as in Step 10. Draw a second line at the opening. Remove the paper and staystitch approximately ⅛″ inside both lines. Cut on the lines.

15. Remove all freezer paper and press all seams in the same direction.

16. Layer the top with the batting and backing; quilt. Trim the outer edges to ¼″ past the star points and bind.

Starry Christmas by Robin Fouquette, 70″ in diameter.
Robin used 12″ blocks instead of starting triangles.

Wild and Crazy Christmas by Jane Hardy Miller, 51″ in diameter

French Braid Borders

Note

Braid border quilts, though not necessarily difficult, are definitely more challenging than the four basic braid quilts shown in Chapter 3 (pages 15–42). You will have better results if you learn the process by making a basic braid first.

Unlike most quilts, the exact size of the center fabric for a French braid–bordered quilt can only be determined after the borders are constructed. This process varies with each project, *but the accurate measurement of both the length and width of your finished braids is critical.* Although I try to avoid using the M-word in deference to readers who are math phobic, some arithmetic calculations are required. However, the individual steps are simple—there are no oddball multipliers, and you are allowed to use a calculator. Just follow the instructions one step at a time.

Border Fabric Selection

The selection of fabric for borders made of French braids is similar to the process for making French braid quilts: the braid run, accents, and starting triangles or center squares come first; the decision for the center of the quilt top follows once the braids are sewn. It is possible that the fabric that inspired the braid run will no longer work once your borders are completed. If that happens, rest assured that you will find something else that looks wonderful—the trick is to get a great braid run in the first place.

First, find a multicolored print from which to select the fabrics for the braid-run borders. Remember that this fabric may eventually appear as a large piece, so pick something you love. Use the colors in this main, inspiration fabric to select and purchase braid-run, accent, and starting triangle or center square fabrics (Chapter 2, page 11). As a very general rule, busy center fabrics need a braid run incorporating calmer prints, or those with less pattern, and vice versa.

To obtain the shorter braid run required for the shorter top and bottom borders of the quilt, some fabrics are eliminated from the run used for the longer side borders. Because the top and bottom border braid runs may no longer start (or end) with the same braid fabric as the side borders, make sure that the starting triangles or center squares look good with most of the braid-run fabrics. The starting triangle or center square fabric can often be used for the ending triangles as well, so if you think you might want to use it later, buy extra now. Just remember that the usual caveat about waiting until the braids are completed to purchase the ending triangle fabric is even more important here, as that fabric must also harmonize with the center medallion fabric.

I prefer not to purchase the original inspiration fabric until after the borders are sewn, because by then another fabric has often become a better choice. (Exceptions: If you can't imagine making the borders without owning a center, if the colors or combination of colors in the inspiration fabric are unusual, if you can't easily visit a quilt shop, if the inspiration fabric is almost gone, or if you love the main fabric enough to want it for your stash even if it doesn't work with the braid borders, buy it now.) After you have sewn the braids, preferably without ending triangles, take them back to the quilt shop, as usual, and look at them with your inspiration fabric. If they still work well together, buy it; if not, try others until you find one that works—it will happen eventually. If you have decided not to use the starting triangle fabric for the ending triangles, select fabric for them and for the inner borders.

I know that this method sounds daunting, but I promise that it is possible—my students do it almost daily. Remember to allow yourself plenty of time and try not to become too emotionally involved with any one fabric or with the process itself. If you are unsuccessful the first time, try again on another day or at another shop—either way, you'll learn a lot about color.

Construction

As with all French braid quilts, the first step is to make the braids (Chapter 3, page 15). For rectangular quilts, the top and bottom borders are usually shorter than the side borders. Because some braid-run fabrics or segments are eliminated in the shorter borders, read the instructions for your chosen project carefully. In most braid border projects, inner borders are treated as separators and sewn to the braids; that unit is then attached to the center portion of the quilt. For some projects, such as *Welcome to New Braunfels, Texas* (page 45) and *Boston Braid* (page 56), the borders require a partial first seam, directions for which appear below.

Sewing Borders with Partial Seams

1. Place the center medallion or block on a flat surface. Place the top or bottom braid border next to one end of the top, with the inner border next to the medallion piece. Align the ending triangle end of the braid border with the side edge of the medallion piece, right sides together, and sew the seam for approximately 6". Press the first 3" of the seam toward the inner border. Gently roll up the dangling braid border and pin it to itself.

2. Find and mark the center of the adjacent edge of the top by folding the end of the center medallion to the edge (or to the marked line) on the partially sewn border.

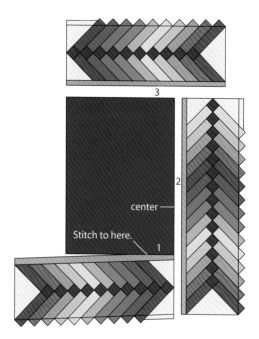

Sew partial first seam and mark the center.

3. Match the centers and ends of a side braid border to the center and ends of the top. Sew the entire seam; press toward the inner border.

4. Repeat Steps 2 and 3 for the remaining 2 borders, adding them counterclockwise around the medallion piece.

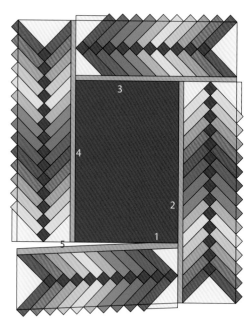

Finish borders.

5. Unpin the first border, match the ends, and sew the rest of the first border seam as in Step 2.

New Braunfels, Texas

Welcome to New Braunfels, Texas by Jane Hardy Miller, 59½″ × 79¼″

Fabric Requirements

Purchase Now

¼ yard each of fabrics 1 and 9 of the braid run—
fat quarters okay

½ yard each of fabrics 2–8 of the braid run

⅝ yard for accent squares

¼ yard nondirectional print for starting triangles—
fat quarter okay

Purchase Later

¼ yard nondirectional print for ending triangles—
fat quarter okay

1¾ yards for center medallion

⅓ yard for inner borders

⅝ yard for binding

4¾ yards for backing, pieced lengthwise

64″ × 84″ batting

Cutting

Refer to pages 15–18 for basic instructions.

BRAIDS: *EITHER* from fabrics 1 and 9, cut 1 strip
8½″ × width of fabric and then cut the strips in half;
OR from fat quarters of fabrics 1 and 9, cut 2 crosswise
strips, each 8½″, from selvage to center. From fabrics 2–8,
cut 2 strips 8½″ × width of fabric; then cut the strips
down to 25″.

ACCENTS: Cut 8 strips 2¼″ × width of fabric. Cut 1 strip in
half and cut the remaining 7 strips down to 25″.

STARTING TRIANGLES: Cut 4 quarter-square triangles,
each with a 13″ base.

ENDING TRIANGLES: Cut 4 squares 7″ × 7″; then cut each
in half diagonally to obtain 8 half-square triangles.

INNER BORDERS: Cut 6 strips 1½″ × width of fabric.

MEDALLION: This is to be determined in Steps 9 and
10. Because seam allowances vary, the size of this piece
may vary. Approximations are given; if your numbers are
extremely different, remeasure and go over the steps again
one by one.

Construction

Refer to pages 19–26 for basic instructions.

1. Separate the braid fabrics into 2 piles. Each pile should
include a half strip each of fabrics 1 and 9 and a 25″ strip
each of fabrics 2–8.

2. From one pile, cut 2 segments 2¼″ wide from each fabric.
Audition the segments with the accent and triangle fabrics;
rearrange or replace as needed. From the same pile, cut 6
more segments from fabric 1, 4 more segments from fabric
9, and 8 more segments from fabrics 2–8.

3. Sew the half strips of accent fabric to fabrics 1 and 9 from
the remaining pile of braid fabrics (page 19). Subcut fabric 1
into 8 segments 2¼″ wide; subcut fabric 9 into 6 segments
2¼″ wide. Sew the 25″ pieces of accent fabric to fabrics
2–8 from this same pile of fabrics. Subcut each into 10 segments 2¼″ wide.

4. Construct the braids (pages 19–20). For all 4 braids, start
with fabric 1 and continue with fabrics 2–9; then follow
with fabrics 8–1. Set 2 braids aside to be the top and
bottom borders. For the remaining 2 braids, which will be
the side borders, continue by repeating fabrics 2–9. Do not
repeat fabrics 1 or 9 where the braid run reverses.

5. Mark the sides and centers of the braids, trim both ends,
and measure the lengths (pages 23 and 25). You will have
2 lengths, one for the longer side braid borders (approximately 67½″) and another for the shorter top and bottom
braid borders (approximately 47½″). If your 2 side borders
are not the same length, take an average. Do the same for
the 2 top and bottom borders. Keep these numbers for use
in Step 7.

6. The marked lines on the right edges of the braids will
become the outside edges of the quilt. Staystitch just inside
the lines on those edges.

7. Sew the inner border strips end to end to obtain enough
length. Cut 2 inner borders the length determined in Step
5 for the side borders; cut 2 inner borders the length determined in Step 5 for the top and bottom borders.

8. Sew the inner borders to the left side of each braid as you
did for separators (page 26), matching ends and centers.
Trim off the zigzag edges on the seamed left sides only
and press the seams toward the inner borders. Measure
the width of the braid borders from the raw edge of the
inner border to the marked line on the opposite braid edge
(approximately 12½″).

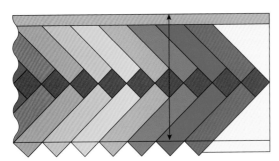

Measure border width, including the inner border.

9. To determine the *cut length* of the center medallion, follow these steps:

a. Subtract the border width (Step 8) from the *side* border length (Step 5).

b. Add ½" to the measurement from Step 9a to obtain the cut length of the center medallion.

10. To determine the *cut width* of the center medallion, follow these steps:

a. Subtract the border width (Step 8) from the *top and bottom* border length (Step 5).

b. Add ½" to the measurements from Step 10a to obtain the cut width of the center medallion.

11. Cut the center medallion fabric the measurement from 9b (approximately 55½") × the measurement from 10b (approximately 35½").

12. Attach the borders, using the partial seam method (page 44.) You may trim the outer zigzag edges on the line now or after you quilt.

13. Layer the top with the batting and backing, quilt, and bind.

Vodka Gimlet by Jane Hardy Miller, 54" × 76"

Monster Mash

Monster Mash by Jane Hardy Miller, 36" × 44½"

Be careful with the fabric selection for this quilt. The accent must be strong enough to carry your eye through the corner background fabric, which may otherwise change from negative to positive space. The 8-fabric braid run consists of 4 fabrics shading from light to dark in one color followed by 4 shading from dark to light in a second color. Fabrics 1 and 8 are used only in the center and corner squares, respectively, and should be nondirectional; fabrics 4 and 5 are eliminated in the top and bottom borders.

◆ Fabric Requirements

Purchase Now

⅛ yard each of fabrics 1 and 8 of the braid run—fat eighths okay

¼ yard each of fabrics 2–7 of the braid run—fat quarters okay

⅜ yard for accent squares

Purchase Later

½ yard nondirectional print for ending and corner triangles

1 yard for center medallion (¾ yard if the print allows crosswise cutting)

¼ yard for inner borders

⅜ yard for binding

1⅜ yards for backing

40″ × 49″ batting

◆ Cutting

Refer to pages 15–18 for basic instructions.

BRAIDS: *EITHER* From fabrics 1 and 8, cut 1 strip 3½″ × width of fabric; then cut the strips in half to obtain 2 strips 3½″ × 20+″ for each fabric. Trim a half strip of each fabric down to 2″ × 20+″; discard the 1½″ strip and then cut the 2″ strips again to obtain 2 strips 2″ × 10+″ for each fabric. *OR* from each fat eighth of fabrics 1 and 8, cut 2 strips from selvage to center—one 3½″ wide and the other 2″ wide; then cut the 2″ strip in half to obtain 2 strips 2″ × 10+″ for each fabric. Keep fabrics 1 and 8 separate from the other braid-run fabrics.

EITHER from fabrics 2, 3, 6, and 7 in the braid run, cut 1 strip 5¼″ × width of fabric. Cut these strips in half to obtain 2 strips 5¼″ × 20+″ for each fabric. *OR* from each fat quarter of fabrics 2, 3, 6, and 7, cut 2 strips from selvage to center 5¼″ wide.

EITHER from fabrics 4 and 5, cut 1 strip 5¼″ × width of fabric; then cut 2 pieces 5¼″ × 10+″ from each strip (you will not use the remainder of these strips). *OR* from each fat quarter of fabrics 4 and 5, cut 1 strip from selvage to center 5¼″ wide; then cut the strips in half.

ACCENTS: Cut 4 strips 2″ × width of fabric. Cut 3 of these strips in half to obtain 6 strips 2″ × 20+″; cut the remaining strip into quarters to obtain 4 strips 2″ × 10+″. Place 2 half strips and 2 quarter strips with fabrics 1 and 8. Place the other 4 half strips with fabrics 2, 3, 6, and 7. Place the remaining quarter strips with fabrics 4 and 5.

ENDING AND CORNER TRIANGLES: Cut 1 strip 5″ × width of fabric. From it, cut 8 squares 5″ × 5″; then cut in half once diagonally to obtain 16 half-square triangles. Cut 1 strip 8″ × width of fabric. From it, cut 2 squares 8″ × 8″; then cut in half twice diagonally to obtain 8 quarter-square triangles.

INNER BORDERS: Cut 4 strips 1½″ × width of fabric.

MEDALLION: This is to be determined in Step 19. Because seam allowances vary, the size of this piece may vary. Approximations are given; if your numbers are extremely different, remeasure and go over the steps again one by one.

 Construction

Refer to pages 19–26 for basic instructions.

Construction of Center Squares and Corner Blocks

1. Sew a half strip of accent fabric to the 3½" half strip of fabric 1; press the seam toward the accent fabric and subcut into 8 segments 2" wide.

Sew and cut strips for center squares. Cut 8.

2. Sew a 2" quarter strip of fabric 1 to each side of a quarter strip of accent fabric; press the seam toward the accent fabric and subcut into 4 segments 2" wide.

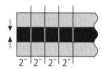

Sew and cut second strip set for center squares. Cut 4.

3. To make a center square, use 2 pieces from Step 1 and 1 piece from Step 2 to make 4 blocks, as shown.

Sew 4 center squares.

4. Repeat Steps 1 and 2, substituting fabric 8 for fabric 1.

5. To make a corner block, use pieces from Step 4 to make 4 blocks, as shown.

Sew 4 corner squares.

Construction of Braid Borders

6. Separate the remaining braid fabrics into 2 piles, with a piece each of fabrics 2–7 in each pile. Place all the accent strips with the second pile.

7. Cut 2 segments 2" wide from each fabric in the first pile and audition with center square and accent fabrics. If satisfied, cut 6 more segments from fabrics 2, 3, 6, and 7 from the first pile; cut 2 more segments from fabrics 4 and 5 from this same pile.

8. Sew a half strip of accent fabric to each of the half strips of fabrics 2, 3, 6, and 7 in the second, uncut pile. Subcut into 8 segments 2" wide (page 19). Sew a quarter strip of accent fabric to each quarter strip of fabrics 4 and 5. Subcut into 4 segments 2" wide.

9. Construct 4 center-out braids, using the blocks from Step 3 as center squares (page 20). Make sure to orient the center square as in the illustration. Use fabrics 2–7 for the side border braid run. Use fabrics 2, 3, 6, and 7 for the top and bottom border braid run.

10. *To the longer side borders only*, add 8 of the 5" half-square-ending triangles (page 20). Leave approximately ¾" of the triangle point hanging off the top of the braid when you sew. (The triangle point may not align with any seamline in the braid as it usually would.)

11. Mark the sides, trim the ends, and staystitch just inside the marked lines on a long side of each side border (page 23). Set aside.

12. Sew a short side of an 8" quarter-square triangle to one end of each (shorter) top and bottom border. Repeat for the opposite ends, orienting as shown. Press the seams toward the triangles.

Add triangles to ends of borders.

13. Sew the remaining 4 quarter-square triangles to the corner blocks from Step 5, as shown. Orient as shown so your accents turn the corners. Press the seams toward the triangles.

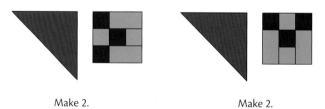

Make 2.   Make 2.

Add triangles to corner blocks.

14. Sew the corners from Step 13 to the borders from Step 12, matching the triangle seams. Make sure that both corners turn in the same direction, as shown in the diagram for Step 18.

15. Sew the remaining 5″ half-square triangles to the corner blocks.

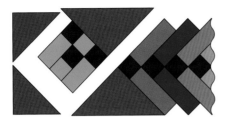

Finish borders.

16. Mark the sides and trim the ends of the top and bottom borders (page 23); staystitch just inside the marked lines on a long side of each border.

Construction of Inner Borders and Center Medallion

17. Measure the *side* borders—the ones without the corner blocks—down the center, from the raw edge at one end to the raw edge at the other end, to find the side border length (approximately 32¼″).

18. For the *top and bottom* border length, measure only the braid section and then add ½″ (approximately 23¾″). Write down these numbers for use in Steps 19 and 20.

Measure.

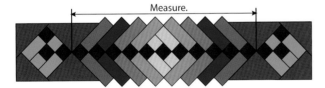

Measure top and bottom borders.

19. Cut 2 inner border strips the exact side border length found in Step 17 (approximately 32¼″). Cut 2 inner border strips the top and bottom border length found in Step 18 *minus 2″* (approximately 21¾″).

20. To determine the *cut length* of the center medallion, subtract 2″ from the length determined in Step 17 (approximately 30¼″). For the *cut width* of the center medallion, use the measurement determined for the inner borders in Step 19 (approximately 21¾″).

21. Pin and sew the 2 shorter inner borders from Step 19 to the top and bottom of the center medallion, matching centers and ends. Press the seams toward the borders.

22. Pin and sew the 2 remaining inner borders from Step 19 to the side braid borders, as you would for separators. Trim the zigzag edges even with the edge of the inner border, as you would for separators (page 26). Press the seams toward the inner borders.

23. Sew the side border units from Step 22 to the center medallion, matching centers and ends.

24. Sew the top and bottom braid borders to the top and bottom of the quilt top, placing the raw edge of the attached inner border on the marked line of the braid border, as you would for separators. Match the centers, ends, and accent points at the corners. Trim the zigzag edges from these 2 seams.

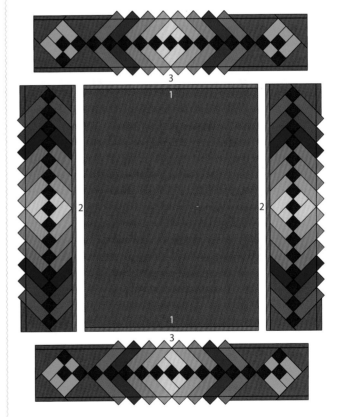

Add borders.

25. You may trim the outer edges of the top on the line now or after quilting.

26. Layer the top with the batting and backing, quilt, and bind.

Flying Free

Flying Free by Jane Hardy Miller, 62¼″ × 84¾″

Fabric Requirements

Purchase Now

⅓ yard each of 11 fabrics for braid run

½ yard for accent squares—fat quarters okay

¼ yard nondirectional print for pieced center squares—fat quarter okay

Purchase Later

2 yards for center medallion

½ yard nondirectional print for corner triangles

⅓ yard for inner borders

⅝ yard for binding

5 yards for backing

67″ × 89″ batting

 # Cutting

Refer to pages 15–18 for basic instructions.

BRAIDS: Cut 1 strip 8¾″ × width of fabric from each fabric in the braid run; then cut the strips in half.

ACCENTS: *EITHER* cut 6 strips 2½″ × width of fabric; then cut 5 of those strips in half. (You will use 9.) Cut the remaining strip into quarters. *OR* from fat quarters, cut 11 strips from selvage to center 2½″ wide; cut 2 of theses strips in half.

CENTER SQUARES: *EITHER* cut 1 strip 7″ × width of fabric and then cut in half. Cut a half strip down to 6½″ × 20+″ and cut the other half strip into 2 strips—one 4½″ × 20+″ and the other 2½″ × 20+″. *OR* from a fat quarter, cut 1 strip from selvage to center in each of the following widths: 6½″, 4½″ and 2½″.

CORNER TRIANGLES: Cut 2 squares 13″; subcut once diagonally to yield 4 half-square triangles.

INNER BORDERS: Cut 6 strips 1½″ × width of fabric.

MEDALLION: This is to be determined in Step 20. Because seam allowances vary, the size of this piece may vary. Approximations are given; if your numbers are extremely different, remeasure and go over the steps again one by one.

  # Construction

Refer to pages 19–26 for basic instructions.

Construction of Center Squares

1. Sew a half strip of accent fabric to the 6½″ half strip of center square fabric, matching long edges. Subcut into 8 pieces 2½″ wide.

Sew strip sets for center squares. Cut 8.

2. Sew a half strip of accent fabric to the 4½″ half strip of center square fabric, matching long edges. Sew the 2½″ half strip of center square fabric to the other edge of the accent fabric. Subcut into 8 pieces 2½″ wide.

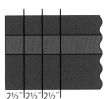

Sew second strip set for center squares. Cut 8.

3. Sew the segments from Steps 1 and 2 into 8 pairs. Rotate half of the pairs as shown; then sew the pairs into 4 squares. Set aside.

Sew pairs into center squares. Make 4.

Construction of Braid Borders

4. Separate the braid fabric half strips into 2 piles, with a piece of each fabric in each pile.

5. Cut 2 segments 2½″ wide from each fabric in the first pile and audition with center square and accent fabrics (page 17). If satisfactory, these 11 fabrics will constitute the braid run for your side borders.

6. While the segments are laid out for auditioning, select 4 to remove from the braid run to create the braid run for the top and bottom borders. Because it is usually easiest to remove segments from the beginning or end of the run, re-audition the new "first" braid-run fabric with the center square. (If you remove fabric from the end of the run, the same fabric will not appear in the corners where the side and top or bottom borders meet.) If satisfactory, the 7 selected fabrics will constitute the braid run for your top and bottom borders. Noting their order, set aside the rejected 4 fabrics from both piles to use in Steps 8 and 9. Cut 6 more 2½" segments from each of the 7 remaining selected braid fabrics.

7. Sew a half strip of accent fabric to each of the remaining halves of the same 7 braid fabrics selected in Step 6. Subcut each into 8 segments 2½" wide (page 19).

8. From the 4 braid fabrics to be used in the side borders only, discard 1 half strip and work only with the other piece. Cut 2 more 2½" segments from each fabric.

9. Sew a quarter strip of accent fabric to the remainder of each fabric cut in Step 8. Subcut each into 4 segments 2½" wide.

10. Use 2 pieced center squares from Step 3 and the segments from Steps 6 and 7 to construct 2 center-out, 7-fabric top and bottom braid borders (page 20), orienting the center square as in the photo.

11. Use 2 pieced center squares from Step 3 and the remaining segments from Steps 6–9 to construct 2 center-out, 11-fabric side braid borders. There are no ending triangles on the borders.

Addition of Inner Borders

12. Mark the sides of the braid borders (page 23).

13. Measure the lengths of the sides of the borders *on the seamlines*. Your marked lines are cutting lines; measure from the intersection of the side seamline (¼" inside the drawn line) and the end seamline (¼" inside the raw edge of the last braid-run fabric). Measure both sides of each braid and write down the numbers. Do this separately for the side and the top and bottom borders.

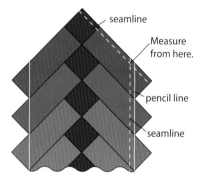

seamline

Measure from here.

pencil line

seamline

Measure sides of braids.

14. Start with the top and bottom braids. Look at all 4 numbers you have written down (a measurement for each side of the 2 top and bottom braids). If they are all the same, use that number (approximately 39½"). If the numbers vary, take an average and use that number. Keep this number to use in Steps 15 and 20. Cut 2 inner border strips the selected length plus at least 3"; fold in half lengthwise and mark the center points in the seam allowances on both edges of the inner border strips.

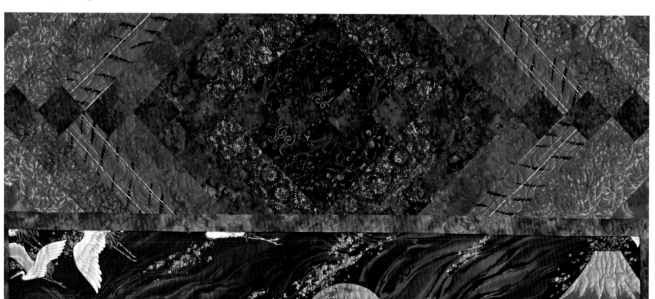

15. Divide the top and bottom braid measurement from Step 14 in half. Beginning at the marked center of the inner border, measure out half the length in both directions and mark in the seam allowances on each end of one long edge. Then mark on each of the opposite long edges ¾″ closer to the center, as shown. Repeat for the second end inner border, using the same measurements.

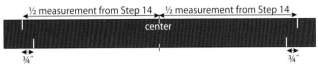

Mark ends of inner borders.

16. Place a braid border flat on a table. Match the outermost marks on the inner border with the intersection of the 2 border seamlines at each end (see the illustration for Step 13). Match the center marks with the point of the center square on the braid. Pin as you would for separators (page 26); stitch the seam from edge to edge. Repeat for the other top and bottom border.

17. Trim the zigzag braid edge even with the edge of the inner border, as you would for separators (page 26); press the seam toward the inner border. Repeat for the other end border.

18. Staystitch the opposite long edge of the braid border just inside the marked line; trim on the marked line.

19. Repeat Steps 14–18 for the side borders (approximately 62″ long).

Cutting Center Medallion and Finishing

20. Subtract 1½″ from each of the border measurements you found in Step 14. Cut your center medallion piece to those measurements. For example, if your border measurements are 39½″ and 62″, cut your center medallion 38″ × 60½″.

21. Refer to Steps 3–5 of Mitered Borders (page 10) to pin, and sew with the borders on top. You should now have a top with a border unit (braid plus inner border) attached to each side.

> **Note**
>
> The border units are not sewn to each other at the corners.

22. Fold as directed in Step 6 of Mitered Borders (page 10). Carefully pin together the last segments of the braid borders, matching ends and accent seams. Sew and press.

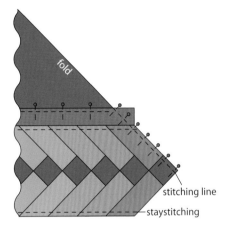

23. Fold the long side of a corner triangle in half and mark. Place it on the diagonal corner edge that was formed by the miter, matching the center mark on the triangle to the center seam on the corner; sew. The triangle is oversized and will hang off the sides; you may square it with the sides now or after quilting.

24. Layer the top with the batting and backing, quilt, and bind.

Boston Braid by Jane Hardy Miller, 93″ × 93″

Fabric Requirements

Purchase Now

⅝ yard each of 9 fabrics for the braid run

½ yard for accent squares

¾ yard nondirectional print for starting and ending triangles

Purchase Later

4¼ yards nondirectional print main fabric for unpieced borders

2½ yards for narrow inner borders, cut lengthwise—includes enough for binding, if desired (1⅝ yards if cut crosswise, binding not included)

¾ yard for binding (if not using same fabric as narrow inner borders)

8¼ yards for backing

97″ × 97″ batting

Cutting

Refer to pages 15–18 for basic instructions.

Because you are cutting several components from the same set of fabrics, it is helpful to place them in separate, labeled groups.

INNER BRAIDS: From fabrics 1–9, cut 1 strip 5¼″ × width of fabric; from each strip, cut 2 pieces 8″ × 5¼″. (The remainder of the strips for fabrics 2–8 will be used for the outer pieced borders.)

OUTER BRAIDS: From fabrics 1–8, cut 1 strip 8½″ × width of fabric; then cut the strips in half. From fabric 9, cut 1 strip 8½″ × width of fabric; from it, cut 2 pieces 11″ and set aside with fabrics 1–8.

OUTER PIECED BORDERS: From fabrics 1–9, cut 1 strip 2½″ × width of fabric. From the leftovers of the 5¼″ inner braid strips of fabrics 2–8, cut 1 strip 2½″ × remaining width of fabric.

ACCENTS: Cut 2 strips 1½″ × width of fabric; subcut into 9 pieces 8″ × 1½″. Cut 5 strips 2½″ × width of fabric. Cut 4 strips in half to make 8 strips 2½″ × 20+″. From the fifth strip, cut 1 piece 11″ wide. (You will not use the remainder of this strip).

STARTING AND ENDING TRIANGLES: Cut 1 strip 7″ × width of fabric; then cut 4 squares 7″ × 7″; cut once diagonally to yield 8 half-square ending triangles.

Cut 1 square 13″ × 13″ and 1 square 8½″ × 8½″; cut each square twice diagonally to yield 4 quarter-square starting triangles each.

Cut 4 squares 5″ × 5″; cut once diagonally to yield 8 half-square ending triangles. Label all the triangle sets.

NARROW INNER BORDERS: *EITHER* cut 17 strips 1½" × length of fabric *OR* cut 35 strips 1½" × width of fabric.

CENTER SQUARE AND UNPIECED BORDERS: These are to be determined in Steps 14, 17, and 18. Because seam allowances vary, the sizes of these pieces will also vary. Approximations are given in parentheses; if your numbers are extremely different, remeasure and go over the steps again one by one.

Construction

Refer to pages 19–26 for basic instructions.

For narrow inner borders: If cut lengthwise, set aside 12 pieces to be used in Steps 26–29; use the remaining 5 pieces as needed. If cut crosswise, cut pieces as needed, seaming end to end when necessary. Press seams open.

Construction of Inner Braid Borders

1. Separate the 5¼" braid fabric strips into 2 piles, with one piece of each fabric in each pile.

2. Cut 2 segments 1½" wide from each fabric in the first pile and audition with the starting and ending triangles and the accent fabric. If satisfied, cut 2 more segments from each fabric in that pile. Note: In the photo, this short braid run begins with fabric 9 and continues in reverse order to fabric 1. Decide which end of your braid run you would like to see at the corners of your center square and begin your braids with that.

3. Sew a 1½" × 8" piece of accent fabric to each fabric in the second pile of braid fabrics. Subcut each into 4 segments 1½" wide.

4. Construct 4 braids (pages 19–20), using only one braid run in each. Start with the 8½" quarter-square triangles and end with the 5" half-square triangles. Leave about ¾" of the triangle point hanging off the edge of the top of the braid, as the point may not align with a seamline as it usually would.

5. Mark the sides, trim both ends, and measure the braid lengths (pages 23 and 25). If all 4 numbers are not the same, pick a number that is close to the average. Keep this number for use in Steps 6, 14, 17, and 18.

6. From the 1½" strips of narrow inner border fabric, cut 4 pieces the length determined in Step 5 (approximately 16½"). Sew a piece to the left side of each braid as for a separator (page 26).

7. Staystitch the braids on the right (unbordered) side just inside the pencil line.

8. Trim the zigzag edges on the bordered sides of all 4 braids as for separators (page 26). Trim the unbordered edges on the pencil line. Set aside.

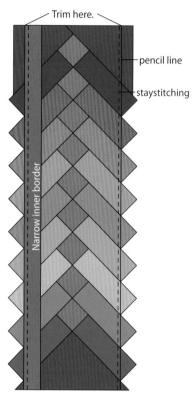

Trim inner braids.

Construction of Outer Braid Borders

9. Use the 8½" strips of braid-run fabric and 2½" strips of accent fabric to sew and cut as for a basic braid quilt—*however* use the 11" piece of accent fabric and the 11" pieces of fabric 9. Cut 8 segments 2½" wide of fabrics 1–8 and 4 segments 2½" wide of fabric 9 from each accented and unaccented braid fabric.

10. Construct 4 braids, beginning with the 13" quarter-square triangles (pages 19–20). Begin with fabric 1 and continue with fabrics 2–9; then follow with fabrics 8–1. (Do not repeat fabric 9 when reversing the order in the braid run.) Then attach the 7" half-square triangles.

11. Mark the sides, trim both ends, and measure the braid lengths (pages 23 and 25) averaging the numbers if necessary. Keep this number to use in Steps 17 and 18.

12. From the 1½" strips of narrow inner border fabric, cut 4 pieces that length (approximately 54"). Sew a piece to the left side of each braid, as in Step 6.

13. Staystitch and trim as in Steps 7 and 8. Set aside.

Construction of the Center Unit

14. To determine the cut size of the center square, first measure the width of your inner braid borders, including the narrow inner border (approximately 8″). Subtract this number from the length determined in Step 5. Add ½″ and cut 1 square this size (approximately 9″ × 9″) from the main fabric. For easier handling, cut a 48″–50″ length from your 4¼ yards of main fabric. Cut your square from a corner; the remainder will be used in Steps 19 and 21 (refer to the diagram with Step 19).

15. Sew the narrow inner border edge of a trimmed braid border from Step 8 to any side of the center square, using the partial seam method (page 44)—*however*, sew only about 2″. Then attach the remaining 3 borders as directed.

16. Measure down the middle of the center unit and cut 2 strips of 1½″ inner border fabric to that measurement (approximately 24″). Sew these strips to the sides of the center. Press toward the narrow borders. Set aside.

17. Determine the size to cut your next unpieced set of borders. To find the *cut length* of the longer pair of unpieced borders:

a. Find the outer braid length from Step 11 (approximately 54″).

b. Measure the width of your outer braid, including the inner border (approximately 12½″), and subtract it from the number in Step 17a to find the finished length of the longer pair of unpieced borders (approximately 41½″).

c. Add ½″ to determine the cut *length* of the longer pair of unpieced borders (approximately 42″).

18. To find the *cut width:*

a. Measure the longer dimension of the center unit (approximately 26″).

b. Subtract the measurement in Step 18a from that in Step 17c to find the *total* unpieced border width needed (approximately 16″).

c. Divide by 2 to find the finished width of each unpieced border (approximately 8″).

d. Add ½″ to find the cut *width* for all 4 unpieced borders (approximately 8½″).

19. From the main fabric piece used in Step 14, cut 2 borders the *exact width* determined in Step 18d × the length measured in Step 18a *plus at least 2″* for the shorter pair of unpieced borders. Cut as shown.

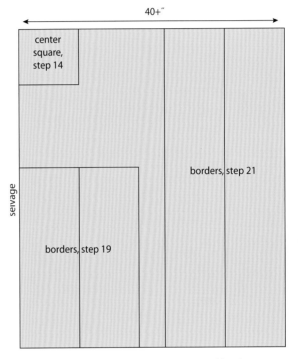

Cutting center square and unpieced borders

20. Cut 2 pieces of 1½″ inner border fabric the length found in Step 18a *plus at least 2″*. Sew 1 inner border strip to a long side of each border piece from Step 19. Press the seams toward the larger pieces; trim to the length found in Step 18a. Sew the inner border edges of these border units to the unbordered sides of the center square unit. Press the seams toward the inner borders.

21. Measure the longer dimension of the quilt across the center. This should be the same number as in Step 17c. From the remainder of the fabric piece cut in Step 14, cut 2 borders this length by the width found in Step 18d. Sew to the remaining 2 sides.

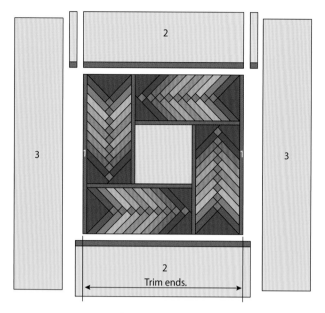

Attach wide unpieced borders.

22. Sew the inner border edges of the 4 outer braid borders to the center square unit, using the partial seam method (page 44). Measure across the center in both directions and set the center piece aside. Keep this number for use in Step 30.

Construction of the Outer Borders

23. Sew together the long edges of the 2½″ × full-width fabric strips of fabrics 1–9, matching the long sides and keeping them in the same order as the braid run. Press the seams in either direction. From this strata, subcut 12 segments 2½″ wide; these will be A segments.

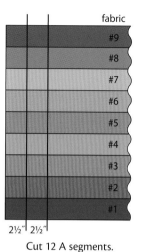

Cut 12 A segments.

24. Sew together and press the 2½″ × partial-width strips of fabrics 2–8, as in Step 23. Subcut into 8 segments 2½″; these will be B segments.

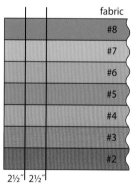

Cut 8 B segments.

25. Use 3 A segments (Step 24) and 2 B segments (Step 25) for each of 4 borders. Sew as shown.

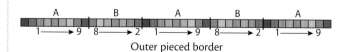

Outer pieced border

You must now prepare the borders for mitering. The remaining multiple borders will be sewn into 4 sets, one for each side of the quilt. When sewing borders together in Steps 26–29, **match the centers, not the ends.** Do not press the seams until Step 29b. If you cut your inner border strips lengthwise, use the 12 you set aside for Steps 26–29.

26. Piece the inner border strips end to end, if necessary, and cut 8 narrow inner borders, each 1½″ × at least 86″. Sew a border piece to each side of the pieced borders from Step 25. The inner border strips are longer that the pieced borders.

27. From the remaining main fabric, cut 4 lengthwise strips 3½″ × at least 80″ and 4 lengthwise strips 6½″ × at least 100″ for the outer borders.

28. Cut 4 narrow inner borders, each 1½″ × at least 80″. Sew a border piece to one side of each 3½″ unpieced border cut in Step 27.

29. Sew the borders together as follows:

a. Sew each bordered pieced unit from Step 26 to the unbordered side of a main fabric border from Step 28. *Be careful:* If you want your pieced border colors to match at the corners of your quilt, 2 borders must begin with fabric 1 on the left ends and 2 borders must begin with fabric 9.

b. Sew a 6½″ border to the remaining raw edge of each bordered pieced unit, matching the centers. Press all the seams in one matching pair of borders toward the 6½″ borders; press all the seams in the opposite direction for the remaining pair.

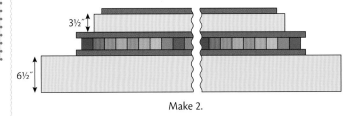

Make 2.

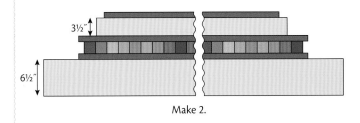

Make 2.

30. Sew 1 border to each side of the quilt using the measurement from Step 22 (page 60) and making sure that the matching pairs are on opposite sides of the quilt.

31. Miter the borders (pages 9–10).

32. Layer the top with the batting and backing, quilt, and bind.

About the Author

Photo by Patricia E. Ritter

Jane Hardy Miller was born and raised in California, where she eventually attended college and law school. Her mother, a home economics teacher, taught her to sew by hand and machine, beginning at age five. Jane made her first quilt in 1968, and for the next ten years, she made about one per year, inventing techniques as she went along. She practiced law briefly in Hawaii and California before moving to Miami in 1979, where she married, had two children, and finally took a beginning quilting class. She has been working and teaching in a local quilt shop since 1987.

Also by
Jane Hardy Miller

French Braid Quilts

Jane Hardy Miller
with Arlene Netten

14 Quick Quilts
with Dramatic Results

For a list of other fine books from C&T Publishing, ask for a free catalog:
C&T Publishing, Inc.
P.O. Box 1456
Lafayette, CA 94549
(800) 284-1114
Email: ctinfo@ctpub.com
Website: www.ctpub.com

C&T Publishing's professional photography services are now available to the public.
Visit us at www.ctmediaservices.com.

For quilting supplies:
Cotton Patch
1025 Brown Ave.
Lafayette, CA 94549
Store: (925) 284-1177
Mail order: (925) 283-7883
Email: CottonPa@aol.com
Website: www.quiltusa.com

Note: Fabrics used in the quilts shown may not be currently available, as fabric manufacturers keep most fabrics in print for only a short time.

Great Titles
from

C&T PUBLISHING

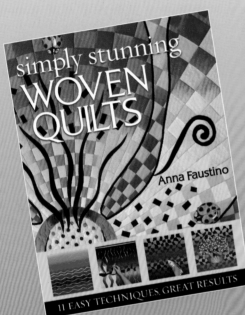
simply stunning
WOVEN QUILTS
Anna Faustino
11 EASY TECHNIQUES, GREAT RESULTS

3-in-1 NEW & IMPROVED
COLOR TOOL
NEW & IMPROVED
3-in-1
COLOR TOOL
NOW INCLUDES THESE MUST-HAVE TOOLS!
• *Numbered* Swatches
• *Two* Value Finders Green and Red
PLUS
• Color Guide
• Fabric Preview Windows
JOEN WOLFROM
IDEAL FOR:
Quilting
Crafts
Home décor
Knitting
Sewing
Scrapbooking
Floral design
Graphic design!

StrataVarious QUILTS
Barbara Persing & Mary Hoover
9 FABULOUS STRIP QUILTS FROM FAT QUARTERS

Machine Quilting Solutions
TECHNIQUES FOR FAST & SIMPLE TO AWARD-WINNING DESIGNS
Christine Maraccini

QUICK & EASY
BLOCK TOOL
QUICK & EASY
BLOCK TOOL
• 102 Rotary-Cut Quilt Blocks in 5 Sizes
• Simple Cutting Charts
• Helpful Reference Tables
IT'S THE QUILTER'S BEST FRIEND!
• Over 500 block options
• Math-free block charts
• Block index
• Mix 'n match blocks
• Handy pocket guide

MARY MASHUTA
Foolproof MACHINE QUILTING
• Learn to Use Your Walking Foot
• Paper-Cut Patterns for No Marking, No Math
• Simple Stitching for Stunning Results

Available at your local retailer or
www.ctpub.com or 800.284.1114